# THE IDEA OF A CHRISTIAN COLLEGE

# THE IDEA OF A CHRISTIAN COLLEGE

Revised Edition

Arthur F. Holmes

WILLIAM B. EERDMANS PUBLISHING COMPANY
GRAND RAPIDS, MICHIGAN / CAMBRIDGE, U.K.

Wm. B. Eerdmans Publishing Co.
2140 Oak Industrial Drive N.E., Grand Rapids, Michigan 49505 /
P.O. Box 163, Cambridge CB3 9PU U.K.

Printed in the United States of America

12  11  10  09  08  07        29  28  27  26  25


**Library of Congress Cataloging-in-Publication Data**

Holmes, Arthur Frank, 1924-
  The idea of a Christian college.
  Bibliography: p. 105
  1. Church and college. 2. Church and college —
United States. I. Title.
LC383.H57    1987      377′.8      86-32825
ISBN 978-0-8028-0258-3


www.eerdmans.com

# Contents

v

# Preface

This revised edition, well over ten years since the book first appeared, results from the helpful and enthusiastic way in which its forebear was received. Colleges across the country have forced me to clarify and correct my ideas, and to address further aspects of the overall subject. The passage of time, moreover, has made my critique of immediate relevance in education less relevant than attention to career preparation.

Chapters 3, 5, 7, and 8 have been revised, chapters 4 and 9 are new, and the sequence has been adjusted. The old chapter 8 has largely disappeared. I have adopted throughout the growing practice, appropriately asked of us by feminists, of trying to avoid one-gender language. That is the least educated language should do to give equal respect to all.

I am grateful to those who have given this effort a fresh start, and in particular Roz Shaw whose mastery of word processing has saved us both a lot of effort. I trust the result will provoke educators, students, and others to good works.

# The Idea
## of a
# Christian College

# 1 WHY A CHRISTIAN COLLEGE?

The French existentialist Jean-Paul Sartre describes the human predicament in the words, "Existence precedes essence." What he intends is that human existence comes devoid of any built-in value, any prior direction or inherent meaning. The naked fact that I am awakens me to the realization that if life is to mean anything at all, then I must myself create its meaning. I am free to make life what I will, dreadfully free, but I can also shrink from this responsibility and lapse into the empty anonymity of "bad faith."

In many basic regards I cannot agree with Sartre, for God has vested life with rich meaning and purpose, and the very fact of my existence is inherently valuable at least to God. I am not free to make of life whatever I will, nor to affirm values wholly alien to the created order. Yet Sartre has highlighted the predicament of the modern mind at a loss to know what life is all about.

Some analogy exists, I suggest, between that existential predicament and the predicament of today's college student. The fact is that too many young people attend college or university, and their parents encourage them, without any gripping sense of what college is all about beyond tentative vocational goals or questionable social aspirations. Many attend Christian colleges for reasons that are so secondary, if not altogether inadequate, that they will end up frustrated unless they can find other meaning to their education, a meaning that is large enough to carry the weight of all that college involves.

The fact also is that public opinion saddles the Christian college with inadequate reasons for existing, reasons the college cannot accept if it is to conceive and implement its task effectively and as a whole. Faulty expectations generate public relations problems and these add a needless burden to the problems of higher education today.

We face a generation of students for whom much in life has lost its meaning, for whom morality has lost its moorings, for whom education has lost its attraction. Add to this the economic crunch on small colleges and it becomes overwhelmingly obvious that we need to get down to basics, to the underlying and central reason for existing at all. Otherwise the student and the college may both lapse in "bad faith" into the faceless anonymity of people and places without distinctive meaning and become mere statistics in the educational almanac.

### AVOIDING PITFALLS

A frequent idea people have of the Christian college has been captured in the label "defender of the faith."[1] Though defending the faith was certainly an apostolic responsibility, it is hard to extend it to all of the educational task, all of art and science or all of campus life. Yet a defensive mentality is still common among pastors and parents; many suppose that the Christian college exists to protect young people against sin and heresy in other institutions. The idea therefore is not so much to educate as to indoctrinate, to provide a safe environment plus all the answers to all the problems posed by all the critics of orthodoxy and virtue.

This is an idea, I say—more a caricature than a reality. The trouble with it is that there often are no ready-made answers, new problems arise constantly, and the critics are perplexingly creative. The student who is simply conditioned to

---

1. This designation was used in the Danforth Foundation study by M. M. Pattillo and D. M. MacKenzie, *Church-Sponsored Higher Education in the United States* (American Council on Education, 1966). The label and description were publicly rejected by a group of Christian colleges.

respond in certain ways to certain stimuli is at a loss when he confronts novel situations, as he will in a changing society undergoing a knowledge explosion. He needs a disciplined understanding of his heritage plus creativity, logical rigor and self-critical honesty, far more than he needs prepackaged sets of questions and answers. The mistake in cloistering young people to keep them from sin and heresy, as evangelicals—of all people—should realize, is that these things come ultimately not from the environment but out of the heart. And while every parent feels protective toward her youngsters, overprotectiveness can stifle faith and hope and love, and trigger opposite excesses of thought and conduct.

Is the idea of a Christian college, then, simply to offer a good education plus biblical studies in an atmosphere of piety? These are desirable ingredients, but are they the essence of the idea? Afer all, through religious adjuncts near a secular campus, students could be offered biblical studies and support for personal piety while they were getting a good education, without all the money and manpower and facilities and work involved in maintaining a Christian college.

Nor is the idea of a Christian liberal arts college to train people for church-related vocations, desirable as this may be as a by-product and central as it may be elsewhere in the educational work of the church. Training, in contrast to education, develops skills and techniques for handling given materials and facts and situations. Education admittedly includes some training in the earlier stages of learning. But the educated person shows independence and creativity of mind to fashion new skills and techniques, new patterns of thought. She has acquired research ability, the power to gather, sift, and manipulate new facts and materials, and to handle altogether novel situations. The educated Christian exercises critical judgment and manifests the ability to interpret and to evaluate information, particularly in the light of the Christian revelation. In a word, if she is to act creatively and to speak with cogency and clarity to the minds of her fellows, the educated Christian must be at home in the world of ideas and people. Christians, unfortunately, often talk to themselves. We think in ruts, and express ourselves in a familiar kind of family jargon. Unless we understand the thought- and value-patterns of our day, as well as those of biblical revelation and the Christian community, and unless we speak fluently the language of our contemporaries, we tragically limit our effectiveness.

Another inadequate reason is the social and extracurricular benefits of the Christian college. It is true that in a small institution one has closer relations with both students and faculty, and that in a Christian institution one expects to find Christian friends and even a life partner. It is also true that one stands a better chance of becoming a campus leader or working in student publications or proving athletic prowess. But these are only fringe benefits; however much they contribute to the student's personal development, they are secondary to education as such. Many of them can be matched outside of college, for it does not take four years out of the work force at a cost of tens of thousands of dollars plus lost earnings in order to play soccer, to chair a committee, to find a mate, to put on a rocking-chair marathon, or even to give Christian witness by serving with love in the local old folks home. These things can be done without ever going to college.

College is for education, the liberal arts college for a liberal education, and the Christian college for a Christian education. These are the basics to which we must get back. To sell college primarily on some other basis is to operate under false pretenses; and to start into college for some other reason is to ask for frustrations. We must therefore come to see education as a Christian calling, we must explore what "liberal education" means and how it is affected by the Christian's task.

Then why a Christian college? Its distinctive should be an education that cultivates the creative and active integration of faith and learning, of faith and culture. This is its unique task in higher education today. While the reality is often more like an *interaction* of faith and learning, a dialog, than a completely ideal integration, it must under no circumstance become a *disjunction* between piety and scholarship, faith and reason, religion and science, Christianity and the arts, theology and philosophy, or whatever the differing points of reference may be. The Christian college will not settle for a militant polemic against secular learning and science and culture, as if there were a great gulf fixed between the secular and the sacred. All truth is God's truth, no matter where it is found, and we can thank him for it all.

Integration also transcends awkward conjunctions of faith and learning in some unholy alliance rather than a fruitful union. What we need is not Christians who are also scholars but Christian scholars, not Christianity alongside education but Christian education. This precludes taking critical potshots at variant interpretations of material without working out a more satisfactory explanation. It shuns tacked-on moralizing and applications, stale and superficial approaches that fail to penetrate the basic intellectual issues. It requires a thorough analysis of methods and materials and concepts and theoretical structures, a lively and rigorous interpenetration of liberal learning with the content and commitment of Christian faith. The Christian college has a constructive task, far more than a defensive one.

## THE EDUCATIONAL DISTINCTIVE

The task is distinctive for two reasons. In the first place it is distinct from other Christian involvement in higher education. The Christian college is of course only one way of making the Christian presence felt academically. In the secular university, Christian students and professors walk a different road, primarily that of witnessing in a non-Christian environment. But important as this is—in fact the Christian college should encourage some of its finest students to become Christian scholars in secular academia—the primary impact is still a *conjunction* of Christian witness with secular education rather than the integration of faith and learning into an education that is itself Christian. The Christian college, moreover, is primarily an undergraduate teaching institution, not primarily a graduate school, nor a collection of professional schools, nor a research and public service institution as the modern university has become. Its task is far more specific.

The Bible institute and Bible college offer another way. They came into being to provide biblical instruction for Christian laymen so as to make their witness and their church work more effective, and they have become undergraduate training schools for Christian workers. They have obvious value, but their function seems to be more conjunctive than integrative. To enlarge a person's biblical and theological knowledge and to train him for Christian service is not the same thing as helping him to work in the arts and sciences and thereby to understand all of life from a Christian perspective.

Programs of biblical studies have recently been established by evangelicals on or near a few secular campuses in order to instruct the Christian and to engage the non-Christian in dialog. These programs range from a Bible-institute type of instruction for undergraduates to graduate-level religious studies offered by scholars who might also teach in the university. But again the impact is primarily conjunctive and only occasionally integrative. Apart from the occasional Christian scholar teaching in a secular university in a nontheological discipline, the integration of faith and learning remains the distinctive task of the Christian liberal arts college.

Some Christian institutions give themselves primarily or largely to professional or vocational training. The seminary, for instance, devotes itself to the professional preparation of college graduates for various types of church-related ministry, and other Christian institutions might focus primarily on vocational preparation in such areas as business education and engineering. We shall comment later about the relation of vocational training to liberal education, but one obvious difference is already apparent: the vocational is more concerned to provide the knowledge and skills needed for a particular set of tasks, while the latter is concerned with other qualities of a liberally educated person and, in a Christian college, with the development of Christian perspectives in all areas of life and thought. What commends the liberal arts college is that the Christian's vocation is larger by far than any specific ministry or vocation one may enter: it reaches into everything a person is and can be or do.

### THE RELIGIOUS DISTINCTIVE

The Christian college is distinctive, in the second place, because we live in a secular society that compartmentalizes religion and treats it as peripheral or even irrelevant to large areas of life and thought. Public education and large segments of private education are consequently thoroughly secular. The Hebrew-Christian worldview that once gave meaning and value to all of Western life and thought has disintegrated. The medieval university was governed by a unifying religious perspective but education today is rootless, or at best governed by pragmatism and the heterogeneity of viewpoints that makes ours both a secular and a pluralistic society. The result is a multiversity not a university, an institution without a unifying worldview and so without unifying educational goals.[2]

The Christian college refuses to compartmentalize religion. It retains a unifying Christian worldview and brings it to bear in understanding and participating in the various arts and sciences, as well as in nonacademic aspects of campus life. Its oldest precedent is the medieval university, where the life and thought of the entire community were penetrated and informed by theological studies.

American higher education was the child of religion, and the history both of church denominations and of the westward expansion can be traced through the history of America's colleges and universities. Harvard, Yale, Princeton, and Columbia—to name but a few—began this way, and the list of those established prior to the Civil War includes forty-nine founded by Presbyterians, thirty-four by Methodists, twenty-

---

2. Clark Kerr, former president of the University of California, uses the term "multiversity" to indicate that it serves a variety of uses in contemporary society, a largely pragmatic notion. See his *The Uses of the University* (Harvard University Press, 1963).

five by Baptists, and twenty-one by Congregationalists.[3] Some of this number have become multiversities or lost their evangelical distinctives, but others are still known among evangelicals today as distinctively Christian colleges, among them Geneva College, Taylor University, and Wheaton. Yet all of them began with an eye to the propagation of religion and morality as well as for the sake of education and culture, and they at least conjoined scholarship with evangelical fervor and a quest for social righteousness, to whatever extent the two were effectively integrated. Over the years, various reasons for existence have been given, sometimes protective or apologetic, sometimes pietist or missionary, sometimes vocational. Yet underlying it all was the basic conviction that Christian perspectives can generate a worldview large enough to give meaning to all the disciplines and delights of life and to the whole of a liberal education.

Some observers have doubted whether the Christian college has any distinctive contribution to make at all, whether it is not too committed to offer a truly liberal education, whether it can survive the skyrocketing cost of private education and the competition of rapidly multiplying state universities and community colleges, or whether the church might not do better to put its resources of people and money behind some other enterprise on the secular campus.

I do not think for a moment that the situation is as bleak as some of these prophets declare, either in terms of our present contribution, or in terms of educational philosophy, or in terms of the economic prospects. I think rather that the Christian college has not sufficiently articulated its educational philosophy, and has not sold the evangelical public or perhaps even its own students and teachers on what it is trying to do. A few exceptions to this generalization have come from denominational schools with well-established views on the relation of Christianity to culture and a well-established scholarly

---

3. D. G. Tewksbury, *The Founding of American Colleges and Universities Before the Civil War* (Columbia University, 1932; Archon Books, 1965), chap. II.

heritage.[4] But by and large we have not dreamed large enough dreams or are confused about the values of liberal education or have forgotten the redemptive impact of faith on culture. In any case we are in integrity compelled to face basic questions. Why should the Christian college exist? Why choose to attend a Christian college? What meaning has Christian liberal arts education today?

---

4. In particular see the Calvin College study, *Christian Liberal Arts Education* (Calvin College, 1970), and the St. Olaf College study, *Integration in the Christian Liberal Arts College* (St. Olaf College Press, 1956), although neither of these is addressed to the general public or to the student.

# 2 THEOLOGICAL FOUNDATIONS

Before we go any further into the idea of a Christian college we must pause and get our theological bearings. As a Christian I am not as radically free as Sartre maintains to do whatever I choose and to create whatever meaning I can for my activities. I am rather committed to thinking and acting as a Christian, that is to say, I will be guided by what I believe about God and his purposes for us. While this is of the utmost importance in shaping ideas aright, it also faces head-on the uneasy feelings some Christians have about higher education—that it is "secular" and "worldly," that it endangers faith and devotion, that it is unimportant in comparison with all our other obligations, or that Christians have no business putting into education the money and energy that could be used to fulfill the missionary mandate of the church.

I have no intention of arguing that the Christian college is our only option. Far from it: we have seen that there are other worthwhile ways in which the Christian presence has been and is being felt in higher education. In fact the Christian liberal arts college is largely an American innovation, unknown in Europe and largely so in Canada. Rather I want in this chapter to unfold the biblical and theological mandate for Christian involvement in higher education in general, as well as for the Christian liberal arts college in particular. The discussion will focus on four concepts: creation, the human person, truth, and the cultural mandate.

*CREATION*

Beginning with the New Testament times and repeatedly since then, the Christian church has been confronted by various kinds of Gnosticism. The Gnostic claimed that we are creatures of two worlds, matter and mind, that matter is the source of life's evils while mind is the source of what is rational and good, and that the two are locked in unending and unresolvable conflict.

Distortions like this often afford occasions for bringing the truth more clearly into focus, and so the apostle Paul, when faced with a Gnostic-like depreciation of bodily things, reminded the church that everything in existence is created by God and therefore is of value (1 Tim. 4:1-5). He might well have had in mind the first chapter of Genesis, in which the term "good" is applied six times to various aspects of creation, and "very good" is finally applied to it all. Thereby God declares that all creation, both the part and the whole, is of value to him; Paul simply adds that as a result it should be valued by us as well. Sin occurs not when we enjoy created things but when we misuse them. The sin, in fact, is in not valuing as we should the resources God has made.

Another kind of Gnosticism has haunted the church in the past, and haunts both church and college to this day. It too claims that we are creatures of two worlds, this time the natural and the spiritual, the secular and the sacred, the world and the church. In each pair of terms the former indicates the source of life's evils, which is to be avoided as much as possible, and the latter is fundamentally incompatible with it. This kind of Gnosticism keeps the Christian from cultural involvement, from artistic appreciation and creativity, from political and social action, and it generates a misdirected fear of science and philosophy and human learning. It produces needless tensions between faith and culture, a defensive attitude and sometimes even outright anti-intellectualism.

Obviously terms like "natural," "secular," and "world" are ambiguous. What is natural for us—like intellectual curiosity and artistic powers and political concerns—is not what the New Testament means by "the natural man," and not everything in this world has the bad moral and religious connotations of the New Testament term "worldly." The forgotten ingredient is that, for all human sin has done to distort the scene, this world is still God's creation, of value to both God and human beings. The "secular" is not itself evil; in fact, in God's world it too is sacred.

The biblical concept of creation imparts sanctity to all realms of nature and to human history and culture. This is my Father's world. To him it owes its existence and order, its developing structures and exciting possibilities. Everything in nature and in history plays its part in carrying out his purposes and in manifesting his glory. For the Christian neither nature nor history is self-originating, self-operating, self-sustaining, or self-explanatory. We therefore approach the works of God, probe their mysteries, and harness their potentialities with humility but with boldness as well. The natural and social sciences lay before us old vistas and new horizons. In the humanities we grapple with ultimate questions and struggle to express our values and beliefs with a precision and beauty becoming the sanctity of this life. To neglect the kind of education that helps us understand and appreciate God's world betrays either shallow thinking or fearful disbelief.

### THE HUMAN PERSON

That God made us in his own image reminds us that in a vast universe that reflects God's glory, humans are uniquely "crowned with glory and honor." We are persons equipped by God with rational, moral, and artistic powers to invest for our Maker. We are sinners also, it is true, whose original image of God and personal powers are corrupted. But we are nonetheless the object of a divine providence that limits evil and preserves human personality, and the object of a divine grace that restores God's image and sanctifies human powers for God's glory.

In other words, we have God-given, God-preserved, God-restorable potential, a potential to be developed, disciplined, and invested in response to God. Such development, discipline, and direction are the Christian's responsibility and stewardship. To educate the whole person, to encourage disciplined learning and the quest for excellence is a sacred trust. The Christian should give himself contagiously to looking around him and to thinking, to the exploration of nature and to the transmission of a cultural heritage, as well as to teaching Christian beliefs and values. The educator's task is to inspire and equip individuals to think and act for themselves in the dignity of persons created in God's image. There is no room here for a dichotomy between what is secular and what is sacred, for everything about people created in God's image belongs to God—that is, it is sacred.

A person is at heart a religious being. I use the word "heart" in its biblical sense in which a person's religious stance is at the "heart" of everything: from it flow all the issues of life. Religion cannot be compartmentalized; the secular mind attempts to do so but succeeds only in fragmenting life, or else rooting another religion at the heart of things, perhaps a quasireligion of a humanistic or materialistic sort.

But if a person is at heart a religious being, then all her activities are animated and informed by her faith, be they intellectual or artistic, political or commercial. There can be no effective dichotomy of the secular and the sacred or of culture and faith. Paul tells us to do everything "heartily, as to the Lord" (Col. 3:23). The phrase is significant, for it is given in response to the Gnostic dualism that had confused the Colossian church by dichotomizing human nature.

Martin Luther once said that the shoemaker should shoe the sole of the pope as religiously as the pope should pray for the soul of the shoemaker. And the astronomer John Kepler: "I have completed a work of my calling with as much intellectual strength as Thou has granted me. I have declared the praise of Thy works to the men who will read the evidence of it, so far as my finite spirit can comprehend them in their infinity."[1] In this sense at least, shoemaking and astronomy, and all our arts and sciences, become religious activities.

---

1. A prayer at the end of *Harmonices Mundi*, 9.

## TRUTH

If we confess that God is the all-wise Creator of all, then he has perfect knowledge of everything we ever sought to know or do. The truth about the physical order is known perfectly to him, the truth about humankind and society, and the truth about everything we ever wondered about in our most perplexed moments. The early church fathers summed this up in what has become a guidepost for Christian scholars ever since—*all truth is God's truth, wherever it be found.*[2]

Once we grasp this principle, then the worlds of literature, philosophy, history, science, and art become the Christian's rightful domain. Of course not everything writers and scientists and others declare can be true; some of it is patently false and some less patently so. Yet truth shows up all over the place, fragmentarily perhaps and with pervasive misinterpretation, and God the Creator is ultimately the source of all that is true.

A second principle is *the unity of truth.* When the apostle writes that in Christ "are hid all the treasures of wisdom and knowledge" (Col. 2:3), he refers not only to divine omniscience but also to what he explained in the previous chapter, that Jesus Christ is God Incarnate, the Creator and Lord of every created thing. All our knowledge of anything comes into focus around that fact. We see nature, persons, society, and the arts and sciences in proper relationship to their divine Creator and Lord. This facilitates an overall philosophy that accords not with pagan principles but with Christ (Col. 2:8). The truth is a coherent whole by virtue of the common focus that ties it all into one.

The Christian college explores truth focused in that way. The pursuit of truth, as pagans like Plato as well as the biblical writers recognized, carries with it certain moral prerequisites: the willingness and determination to learn, intellectual honesty, a self-discipline that makes lesser and more

---

2. See further my *All Truth is God's Truth,* (Eerdmans, 1977; reprint, InterVarsity Press, 1983).

selfish satisfactions wait. But while such dedication is prerequisite to learning, a Christian understanding of things is not thereafter achieved by some mystical illumination unrelated to rational considerations. The Holy Spirit illuminates the Christian mind by witnessing to the truth taught by the Scriptures, not independently thereof and not without the intellectual work involved in studying the biblical revelation and understanding Christian theology.

The Christian regards the biblical revelation as the final rule of faith and conduct, but he does not think of it as an exhaustive source of all truth. The teaching authority of Scripture commits the believer at certain focal points and so provides an interpretive framework, an overall glimpse of how everything relates to God, but there is no royal road to learning and no alternative to disciplined intellectual inquiry if we would find out about nature or man or God. Moreover, if all truth is God's truth and truth is one, then God does not contradict himself, and in the final analysis there will be no conflict between the truth taught in Scripture and truth available from other sources.

The relation between reason and revelation is therefore in principle no more antithetical than the relation between culture and the church. That God has revealed himself in Scripture means among other things that he has given us a true and reliable source of knowledge, sufficient for its intended purposes, but we cannot understand that revelation and grasp the knowledge it imparts without thinking about it. Revelation by whatever means affords a source of knowledge and an impetus to learning; reason is a God-given capacity for understanding and organizing and using what is revealed. Revelation and reason are both God-given, both to be valued and used.

Faith is neither a way of knowing nor a source of knowledge. Faith is rather an openness and wholehearted response to God's self-revelation. It does not preclude thinking either about what we believe or about what we are unsure of, nor does it make it unnecessary to search for truth or to examine evidence and arguments. Faith does not cancel out created human activities; rather it motivates, purges, and guides them. It devotes "all my being's ransomed powers," including reason, to God. Like any gift the intellect can be misused, but it is still God's gift, intended by him to be fully enjoyed and rightly appropriated within the context of a living faith.

Christian commitment does not restrict intellectual opportunity and endeavor, but rather it fires and inspires purposeful learning. Christian education should not blindfold the student's eyes to all the world has to offer, but it should open them to truth wherever it may be found, truth that is ultimately unified in and derived from God. It should be a liberating experience that enlarges horizons, deepens insight, sharpens the mind, exposes new areas of inquiry, and sensitizes our ability to appreciate the good and the beautiful as well as the true.

What I have said about truth and intellectual inquiry could be said also about goodness and the concern for social justice. All goodness, justice, love, and every virtue come ultimately from God. Every good thing comes from the Father, and St. Paul therefore encourages us to think about "whatsoever things" are just and virtuous as well as true (Phil. 4:8).

Something similar can be said for the beautiful and for the creative arts, for Paul adds the lovely or "pleasing" to the true and the good. Certainly God created our capacity for aesthetic enjoyment, he made the world that delights and awes us, and he made us artistically creative. In this sense, then, all beauty and creativity is God's, to be enjoyed and dedicated to him. None of our cultural endeavors is excluded, nor can they be from education that is Christian.

## THE CULTURAL MANDATE

At creation God made us in his own image, to steward our own and nature's resources creatively and wisely. Our cultural responsibilities originate here. Tensions occur between faith and culture, it is true, some of which are due to our inability to grasp relationships and see life's task as a whole, and others of which are due to the imperfections of particular cultures. Nothing in this cultural mandate makes twentieth-century

American culture, or any other culture, sacrosanct; every culture stands constantly under the judgment of God. But cultural responsibilities persist; they began with creation.

We read in Scripture of the agriculture and art and technology that people developed, of the cities they built and the nations of which they were part. We read of social justice and compassion provided for in the Jewish law, preached by the prophets, and practiced at times by the kings. We read of the virtue of conscientious work, the joys of song and of love and friendship. We read the Old Testament poetic books whose artistic form is that of their culture. In the New Testament we meet one who incarnated himself in the mundane, in the social and religious and political structures of the time. He spent thirty of his thirty-three earthly years in "secular" pursuits, in the family at Nazareth and at the carpenter's bench. From the parables he told we sense his delight in nature and in Jewish culture. He says that all of life is a stewardship, sacred before God. We meet the apostles who talk of the Lordship of Christ in everything, and in their missionary work use cultural vehicles, even Greek philosophical concepts, to communicate the gospel.

We are cultural beings. God made us to be that way and there is no escape from cultural involvement and cultural tasks. Even a counterculture itself becomes a culture, or else it blends back into the culture it condemns. Occasionally a religious community tries to stand outside culture, but it develops into a subculture with its own cultural tasks.

Culture was ordained by God. The creation mandate to replenish and subdue and have dominion has never been rescinded. It may be argued that sin changes things and perverts culture, so that God's grace calls us out of culture to witness to it rather than participate in it. Yet the biblical cases of cultural involvement all occurred after the fall. In fact Psalm 8 defines human uniqueness in terms of the cultural mandate given in Genesis 1, and Hebrews 2 reiterates the Psalmist's words. In response to the complaint that humankind has sinned and thereby failed culturally, the epistle to the Hebrews speaks of the redemptive work of Christ, later of those who did wide varieties of things "by faith" (Heb. 11), and of the believer's relationship to such cultural things as marriage and money and political authority (Heb. 13).

The point is that God's goodness as well as human sin affects culture. Theologians speak of the "common grace" of a God who makes the sun to shine on the just and the unjust alike, and preserves among fallen people a measure of civil justice and social order and a degree of human love and compassion. Fallen people, whether they want it or not and however distortedly, still image their Creator. The mathematical genius of an Einstein and the artistic creativity of a Picasso are God's gifts to humankind through common grace.

But God's redeeming grace also affects culture, for the people he makes whole are cultural beings whose activities are now directly affected by the truth and love of God. They bear witness by their lives, and that includes their arts and sciences and their politics, to the God in whose image they are being re-created. God's grace affects a culture through the cultural penetration of those his grace redeems.

To confess God as Creator and Christ as Lord is thus to affirm his hand in all life and thought. It is to admit that every part of the created order is sacred, and that the Creator calls us to exhibit his wisdom and power both by exploring the creation and developing its resources and by bringing our own created abilities to fulfillment. For while all nature declares the glory of God, we human beings uniquely image the Creator in our created creativity. Implicit in the doctrine of creation is a cultural mandate and a call to the creative integration of faith with learning and culture. It is a call, not just to couple piety with intellect, nor just to preserve biblical studies in our school, but more basically to see every area of thought and life in relation to the wisdom and will of God and to replenish the earth with the creativity of human art and science.

Plainly, the four theological concepts we have considered affect the values we find in education and liberal learning. To reject these values is to flirt with Gnosticism. The Christian college accepts and helps to realize them in the lives of its students. All of life with its culture and its learning must be penetrated with Christian perspectives, if Jesus Christ is to be Lord of all. All of a young person's human potential must be as fully developed as possible, if the stewardship of his or her life is to honor God. The Christian has a mandate in education.

# 3 THE LIBERAL ARTS: WHAT AND WHY?

A typical college student sat in my office. He had come to preregister, and beneath his hesitation I detected confusion about the purpose of education. Should he take another literature course, or something in accounting? Why the history of philosophy or of art, or of anything else for that matter? He was majoring also in psychology, but why experimental psychology or personality theory when what he wanted was to understand people so as to communicate more effectively? What would he ever do with all this stuff anyway: literature, history, philosophy, experimental psychology? Whatever use does it have in "real life," and in particular for the Christian?

I could have taken several approaches. I could have asked, Socratic style, "What do you mean by *real* life?" And I might have led him to see that literature and history and philosophy and psychology deal with reality to a larger extent and in deeper dimensions than any collection of "how to do it" courses. I could have talked about the cultural mandate under which the first task to which God's grace has restored us as Christians is to glorify God in all our creatureliness, and therefore to understand the creation and with heart and mind to join in the cultural undertaking of the human race. I could simply have pontificated that this is a liberal arts college and he should get a liberal education. But not being sure he would understand the implications of that, I suggested that his was the wrong question to ask about education.

## ASKING THE RIGHT QUESTION

We are reminded by those who try to buffer us against "future shock" that our present job-skills will soon be outmoded, and that the things we learn to do now will be vastly different in a few short years. Education should therefore prepare us to adapt, to think, to be creative. Whether these prophets exaggerate or not, it is also true that the "I" who in a few short years will "do something in real life" will by then be a different "I" from the "I" who now takes a course in college. My personality is not static but dynamic, growing, changing. The question to ask about education, then, is not "What can I do with all this stuff anyway?" because both I and my world are changing, but rather "What will all this stuff do to me?" This question is basic to the concept of liberal education.

When I began to teach, someone reminded me that the verb "to teach" carries a double object. Teaching is like telling: I have just told a story about a student, but I have also told you. When people ask what I teach, I sometimes say "philosophy," but sometimes (and partly to tease them) I say "students." For the question a teacher must ask about his teaching is not "What can they do with it?" but rather "What will it do to them? What sort of men and women will they become by wrestling with this material in the way I present it? And what sort of materials and methods could I develop to help them become more fully the people they are capable of being?"

Now this "whatever-can-I-do-with-all-this-stuff" question comes up in various disguises. Perhaps the most frequent is the vocational: what will history and literature and philosophy contribute to my work as a businessman, a doctor, an engineer, or a minister? Liberal education contributes far more than is sometimes supposed to many vocations, and more will be said of this later. Moreover, we must never underestimate the importance of work; its value in the order of creation is far greater than the value of earning a living. A person's daily work, whatever it is, should be an offering to God (Eph. 6:5-9), as well as a service to others and a means to one's own personal growth and dignity. This biblical approach to work is vastly different from the aristocratic attitude of Aristotle and some of the Greeks who unduly elevated the life of the mind in contrast to more mundane tasks. But to realize this is to uncover the fallacy in a purely vocational approach to education. The human vocation is far larger than the scope of any job a person may hold because we are human persons created in God's image, to honor and serve God and other people in all we do, not just in the way we earn a living.

None of us wants the kind of dehumanized brave new world that manufactures men and women to fill jobs. Our technological society has been indicted for making productivity the purpose of society, rather than people. Yet the same indictment could be leveled against the view that education is job training, for it too has sold out to the productivity principle by subordinating what people are to what they do. A person is not just *homo faber,* one who makes things. If he were just a worker, vocational training would suffice; but since he is more than a worker it follows that vocational training is not enough.

Vocations and jobs are made for people, not people for vocations and jobs. The question to ask about an education is not "What can I do with it?" but rather "What is it doing to me—as a person?" Education has to do with the making of persons, Christian education with the making of Christian persons. Since this is what God's creative and redemptive work is about—the making of persons in his own image—it follows that an education that helps make us more fully persons is especially important to Christians.

### DEFINITIONS

What is liberal education that makes it larger and more enriching than vocational preparation? What do we mean by the liberal arts? A term may be defined by its extension or by its intension. To define by extension, we identify the class of particular things to which a term refers. The term "person" extends to Tom, Dick, Harry, Mary, Jane, Sue—the whole gamut. To define by intension, we try to capture the concept involved, the underlying nature that all members of that class have in common, the essence of it.

An extensional definition of the liberal arts would refer to a set of academic disciplines. In the Middle Ages the term referred to a trivium plus a quadrivium of disciplines. The initial three concerned the art of language and were grammar, rhetoric, and logic; the four (geometry, arithmetic, music, and astronomy) were regarded as essentially mathematical and taught the art of reasoning and abstract thought.

So the liberal arts were a group of disciplines having to do with language and thinking, and something of the intension of the term emerges as a result. Along with these liberal arts were disciplines like theology and law, which not only equipped people to serve God and society but also provided the subject matter for their rational inquiry. Theology and science rapidly became part of the liberal arts. By the time we get to the eighteenth and nineteenth centuries, the extension of the liberal arts broadens and becomes synonymous with classical education, so that you are not liberally educated without Latin and Greek and classical literature, and unless you can write Latin poetry and give speeches in classical languages. For a while it included natural philosophy (science), moral philosophy (ethics and political science), and mental philosophy (logic and metaphysics), so that to this day the "Doctor of Philosophy" degree can be earned in almost any discipline. In the twentieth century, there has been a tendency to equate the liberal arts with a broad, general education that ranges across the natural sciences, the social sciences, and the humanities, and religion is increasingly considered as one of the liberal arts.

Whatever the disciplines cited, extensional definitions are insufficient. They refer to the changing content of human knowledge rather than to the purpose for which one learns, so that students still ask, "Why do we have to learn this stuff anyway?" and "Why is this important?" If liberal education is equated with general education, then the liberally educated person is one who has dabbled in a promiscuous variety of things. Such a scope is insufficient either to fully motivate students or to justify itself, because it is hopelessly fragmented. It might allow the principle that all truth is God's truth wherever it is found, but it disregards the unity of truth. It does nothing to unify a person or his view of life, and it might well encourage the conclusion that life has no overall meaning at all. It simply creates a connoisseur of the fragments of life. But a jack of all trades is a master of none, a fragmented individual. What today we label as general education requirements do not themselves make for the unified understanding that education desires.

To see what we mean by liberal education we have to get beyond extensional to intensional definitions and grasp the unifying essence of the thing. Cicero suggested that liberal education is the education of free men for the exercise of their freedom rather than of slaves. Aristotle leaves the impression that education is for the wise use of one's leisure, for free men are leisured men who do not have to work but are in a position to exercise political and social leadership. In that sense liberal education becomes education for leadership, and in that spirit the early American college emphasized preparation for the leadership exercised by the professions, hence a nonprofessional preparation for the professions through developing one's rational powers. More recently the stress has been on education for citizenship in a democracy. Here again the conception is of a free people and the role they must play in life beyond their remunerative work.

In all of this, the needed clue is that the liberal arts are those which are appropriate to persons as persons, rather than to the specific function of a worker or a professional or even a scholar. A person may be all of these things, but she is more basically a person. It was Cicero who defined the liberal arts as those which are appropriate to humanity. If one is to be anything more than a specialist or technician, if one is to feel life whole and to live it whole rather than piecemeal, if one is to think for himself rather than live secondhand, the liberal arts are needed to educate the person. There is no difficulty in transferring this clue concerning liberal education to a Christian conception of persons created in the image of God. We are to image God in all of our creaturely activities, our cultural existence and every phase of our humanity. To image God in the fulness of our humanity is our highest calling. A liberal education that develops this stewardship of all we are therefore implements God's calling, and the creation mandate finds expression in the educational process.

In his classic nineteenth-century work, *The Idea of A University,* John Henry Newman distinguishes between liberal and useful arts. It is not a complete disjunction, for the liberal arts are also useful, and the useful arts are often based on liberal arts and sciences. But the point is that some arts are more liberal than others, and some more useful for economic and other particular purposes than they are of value to us in themselves. The distinction is worth preserving. It is the distinction between intrinsic and instrumental value. Some things have little but instrumental value; for example, a shining new coin with the head of George Washington on one side and the American eagle on the other has instrumental worth: it is good for what you can buy with it but little else. If you tell me it is of intrinsic worth and you value it for itself, I call you a miser. Other things have far more intrinsic worth as well as some instrumental value. Understanding is valued for itself. Beauty and goodness are of value in themselves. In addition to the fact that beauty may have some utilitarian function and that it pays to be good and that knowledge can be useful, in addition to their instrumental worth, is their intrinsic worth. Liberal learning concerns itself with truth and beauty and goodness, which have intrinsic worth to people considered as persons rather than as workers or in whatever function alone.

We may distinguish along these lines between literature as one of the liberal arts and journalism, in which the use of what is written predominates; between the natural sciences as a quest to understand nature, which is liberal learning, and the technology that does something else with it; between political science on the one hand as the attempt to understand political institutions and processes, and propaganda techniques on the other; between the science of psychology and the useful art of counseling; between theology and the work of evangelism; between philosophy as a liberal art and apologetics as one use it might have. Usefulness is no crime. But the practical uses of things we learn are limited and changeable, while the effect of learning on the person is less limited because it lasts. Liberal learning therefore takes the long-range view and concentrates on what shapes a person's understanding and values rather than on what he can use in one or two of the changing roles he might later play.

The question to ask about education is not "What can I do with it?" That is the wrong question because it concentrates on instrumental values and reduces everything to a useful art. The right question is rather "What can it do to me?"

### WHAT IS A PERSON?

Starting with this clue, what do the liberal arts contribute to the making of a person? This depends on the prior question: "What is a person?" Here the Christian and the Christian college must be extremely careful. If you take a Freudian or a Marxist or a pragmatist or a behavioristic view of persons, your conception of education will be geared accordingly. What then is a person? Three features, I suggest, are essential for Christian higher education.[1]

First, a person is *a reflective, thinking being*. I use the term "reflective" to avoid Enlightenment connotations of "reasoning" that is unimpassioned and uncommitted, detached and neutral on matters of faith and value, insisting on logical demonstration, a mind ruled by reason alone, and ruling all of nature and society by the power such reason provides. On the contrary we are finite beings, we "see through a glass darkly" and "know in part," and we are not in the final analysis ruled by just what we know. Yet, as Aristotle said, by our very nature we desire to know, we are inquisitive, we wonder and we imagine, we take things apart and we try to put things

---

1. For a fuller elaboration of this view of persons, see my *Contours of a World View* (Eerdmans, 1983), chap. 7.

together. We want to know what makes things work, what life is all about, what we can do about it, and what we can hope for. And such thinking has a far-reaching influence in our own lives and beyond.

Too often God-given imagination and curiosity are stifled in early education, or thinking is regarded as an impious spectator sport. The first task of liberal education is to fan the spark and ignite our native inquisitiveness.

To be reflective is to be analytic. Inquisitiveness leads us to examine more and more closely what is going on. "How does this happen? What do you mean? How can this be?" Thinking is asking what and why and how. It asks about the meaning of life and probes the mysteries of our existence. It seeks understanding. We have to ask questions and probe, we have to learn to think and to think critically for ourselves because this is part of what it is to be human.

To be reflective is also to see things in relationship, to organize ideas into an ordered whole, to be systematic, to work toward a unified understanding. Three educational implications follow. First, interdisciplinary approaches to learning are important. Second, theoretical questions are unavoidable because humans alone in creation are theorizing beings who extrapolate beyond the known and speculate about the unknown, formulate hypotheses for science to explore, and imagine new worlds for art to create. Third, worldviews must be examined and shaped, for we still strive to see things whole, however imperfectly we envision that unity of truth which we seek.

Bertrand Russell suggests that education has two purposes: to form the mind and to train the citizen. The Athenians, he says, concentrated on the former but the Spartans on the latter. The Spartans won but the Athenians were remembered. To form the mind, to stretch the understanding, to sharpen one's intellectual powers, to enlarge the vision, to cultivate the imagination and impart a sense of the whole—this is the task of liberal education.

If God, too, is rational and if we struggle within the limitations of our creatureliness to think God's thoughts after him, then the reflective life has religious significance. Like all of human existence, it has religious roots and proceeds from the heart; in the final analysis it is a person's religion that unifies her understanding. To the Christian in the Christian college, then, the development of an inquiring mind becomes an expression of faith and hope and love addressed to God. It is part of our response to God's self-revelation.

Intellectual development requires that we read and write. Reading is of course prerequisite to informed conversation, an art that is often sadly underdeveloped today. Writing is prerequisite to exactness of thought and expression. Together they accomplish what "discussion" alone can never achieve, unless it is constantly monitored and analyzed by an unusually competent teacher who forces the discussants to think and then to reshape their thoughts in more and more consistent and cogent and lucid ways. To read is to gain input, to fertilize imagination, to conceptualize, to follow an argument, to evaluate. To write is to become articulate, to express what I feel and explain why I feel as I do, to expound, to argue, to offer good reasons, to explore relationships, to have a sense of the whole, to see things in total context. To teach a person to read and to write is to teach him to think for himself, to develop more fully the possession of his God-given powers. He becomes in fact, not just in possibility, a reflective, thinking being.

Second, a person is a *valuing being*. We make value judgments and act to realize our values. The theological foundations of the last chapter brought the value of higher education into focus. A worldview that ties our thinking together and gives direction to what we do is not simply a theoretical system of value-neutral propositions, but a valuational orientation to life. It expresses what we hope as well as what we think; it says what we love and what we desire. A person who values the truth speaks it; one who values social justice works for it; if one has hope amidst life's turmoil, then life has meaning. We value peace and justice, love and beauty, community and solitude. We express our values in our arts and sciences, our political life and social institutions, in the very history we create. In the humanities—literature, the arts, philosophy, history—human values become explicit. The value a writer places on various aspects of life comes out in the literature he writes. Read Hemingway or Tolstoy or Brecht and grapple with their views, for literature and the arts are a laboratory of life: one does not need to experiment with drugs and sex and violence in order to understand life's experiences and emotions for oneself.

Values are more than feelings. By now the emotivist theory of value should be dead and can be buried, for it has been taken to pieces by philosophers who have shown beyond doubt that valuing also involves reasons that can be argued and generalized. Yet experience-oriented young people still seem to reduce values to feelings: a thing is right that you feel right about. It is "right for me." The result, as C. S. Lewis shows in his *Abolition of Man,* is a thorough relativism. For the Christian theist, values are more than feelings and they are not all relative; they have their basis in the very nature of what a person is in God's creation and so in the wisdom and the will of God. We image our Creator as valuing beings, for he, too, values: he loves, he delights, he seeks to realize the values he invested in his creation, and our values must follow from his.

Another educational goal accordingly follows, to teach values as well as facts. Somewhere in the curriculum, the student should be exposed to ethics, to social problems, to aesthetics and other areas of value, and to the logical structure of value judgments. How do I make a moral judgment that is not a simple case of black and white, of obvious right or wrong? Are the consequences of an action all that matters (its instrumental value) or are some things intrinsically better than others? In a Christian college one must come to see the distinctive ingredients and bases of Christian values, and will, one hopes, make those values one's own.

Third, a person is a *responsible agent,* accountable ultimately to God, for life is after all a stewardship of what God has created. This in fact seems to be the purpose in our reflective and valuing capacities, for understanding and right values are prerequisite to responsible action. Moreover we are responsible agents in every relationship, whether with other people or the physical world of which we are part, or with God himself. Friendships, marriage and family, work and recreation, political involvement and social action, art and technology, spiritual life and church activities—all of these call for understanding and right values. They need reflection informed by natural and social science and by the insight and sensitivity about human affairs which the humanities afford. They require judgments about ethical and aesthetic values, or political and economic goods, always in relation to that highest end which is to glorify God with heart and mind and strength.

This is where a sense of history is important; for people (including people who have been college students) shape history for better or for worse. We are in fact history-makers by the way our actions contribute to the future of the church, the family, the nation, the economy, or to the unfolding of art and science. Two educational goals follow. One is a critical appreciation of the past. Appreciation grasps the continuity of a heritage from the past into the present. But I say "critical appreciation" because unless we see the limitations of our past we will never be motivated to transcend those limitations in shaping our future. Critical appreciation of the past—whether in national politics, or in art and music, or in the church—will free us from the present to see creative possibilities for the future. The other goal is therefore creative participation in the future. For college is a place of learning, of preparation, and liberal education helps people develop a sense of direction growing out of roots in the past, it helps shape far-sighted and good goals, it can lead to intelligent, creative, strategic action.

We can represent this view of the person and of liberal education in the following diagram. To be responsible agents (A) in all of life's relationships ($R_1$ . . . $R_5$) presupposes our development as reflective (R) and valuing (V) beings.

Perhaps other aspects of human nature should be considered as well. We have not distinguished a person's religious nature for, as we pointed out in Chapter 2, it is the very heart of our being from which everything else stems. The religious

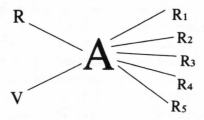

dimension of life is lived in and through the reflective life, the valuing and the responsible activity in which we engage.

What of the physical and the social? They are included in the relationships of which we have spoken. The physical provides a necessary if insufficient condition for all a person is and does in this life, and it should be valued and developed accordingly. But by definition, liberal education should concern itself with physical education as with other curricular areas in relationship to the goals of liberal education. That is, the primary concern will not be with physical skill or strength or stamina, but with the development of the person—emotional balance and self-understanding, the ability to act decisively and creatively, one's values. The measure of a person is neither athletic prowess nor the lack thereof. It is other characteristics that make one truly human. Physical training will not automatically either enhance these characteristics or detract from them, although it can contribute in either direction. Plato said that excessive emphasis on athletics without literature or philosophy produces a pretty uncivilized type with no use for reasoned conviction, whose life is one of clumsy ignorance unrelieved by grace or beauty; whereas a purely academic life without athletic training leaves one with little backbone. He seems on the right track, but he forgets that some sports are also arts, creative and beautiful, so that the athlete may well learn to understand and appreciate aesthetic values rather than simply acquiring strength, skill, self-reliance, and a team spirit. In any case the Christian college must not only value highly the body God made but will also teach physical education in a humanizing and liberating way, if the values are aesthetic or moral and social, or if the end-product is decisive action based on carefully argued plans.

A person's social nature must be cultivated without drifting into the extremes of individualism or collectivism. More will be said of this later. The social, like the physical, is a necessary but insufficient precondition for reflective, valuing beings and their responsible action. Rational inquiry is not carried on in isolation but in dialog with other minds of the past and present: because it builds on their work, it is a social undertaking. In large measure we acquire our values from parents and peers and others, we implement them in whatever social groups we belong to, and we seek to transmit them to others. To that extent at least, the goals of liberal education will include not only self-understanding, but also an understanding of other people and of social institutions and processes. This is essential in preparing men and women for participation in society, whether through marriage or through citizenship activities or through business and professional relationships.

Liberal education is an open invitation to join the human race and become more fully human. Its general goals include the ability to read and write and thereby think independently, an appreciation of lasting values coupled with the ability to make sound value judgments and live by them, a critical appreciation of the past and responsible creative participation in the future. Generalizations of this sort can readily be translated into objectives for different disciplines, so that the science professor will stress an understanding and appreciation of methods and concepts, and the historical development of his science and its cultural ramifications, rather than stressing technique alone or making the student into a narrow specialist. A considerable degree of specialization is of course appropriate in any major field of concentration, sufficient to prepare the student for graduate work in a highly competitive situation, but the liberal arts college has no business producing narrow specialists who see no further than their laboratory, have no larger sense of responsibility, and little understanding of science as an essentially human cultural undertaking. It would be inexcusable nowadays for a Christian college to teach science without discussing the moral and social problems it has raised. Similarly the art teacher will work toward an understanding and appreciation of the creative process, of aesthetic values and the history and social role of art, for artists like scientists can become narrowly specialized technicians rather than responsible human beings.

Liberal education provides an opportunity to steward life more effectively by becoming more fully a human person in the image of God, by seeing life whole rather than fragmented, by transcending the provincialism of our place in history, our geographic location, or our job. Provincialism isolates us from our past, isolates us from segments of the human race; cultural provincialism isolates the American way of life from anything else; vocational provincialism limits the horizon to a certain kind of task. But liberal education is an opportunity to become whole and to see life whole rather than provincially fragmented in one way or another. It is an opportunity to find meaning for everything I am and do. Christian liberal arts education is concerned that we do this in the light of God's self-revelation, so that we learn to think Christianly, to value as Christians should, and so to act responsibly. I would think it worthwhile if a student, when asked what he learned in college, could reply, "I learned what it is to see and think and act like the human person God made me to be."

If the person, including what she becomes in this life, has an eternal destiny, then what I become in the process of education lives forever. In that sense I can take with me some of the benefits of a liberal education, while the benefits of vocational training last only for the duration of the job for which it equips me here and now. Christian liberal arts education has an eternity in view.

# 4 LIBERAL ARTS AS CAREER PREPARATION

The what-can-I-do-with-it question about the liberal arts crops up repeatedly in people's minds, especially in harder economic times. While some colleges have succumbed to these pressures and have vocationalized their curricula, other educational, business and professional leaders have reaffirmed the importance of liberal learning for career preparation. To be sure, as we have already remarked, there is more to life than work: a forty-hour job is less than a quarter of the hours in any week, and little more than a third of one's waking hours. Why then should we not also be educationally concerned about the other three-quarters or two-thirds?

Perhaps more directly significant is the fact that most freshmen do not yet know themselves or their abilities or the options available well enough to make a sensible vocational decision. This is borne out when we realize that two-thirds of all students change their career plans at least once, often twice, in their four years of college, and most graduates change jobs at least once in the first five years after college. Moreover, who knows what the job market will be like ten or even four years from now? Popular fields quickly get overcrowded and then reopen as the demographics change. Shifting markets and developing technology make once-needed skills obsolete. All this means that a purely vocational training is too shortsighted as well as too narrow.

On the other hand a liberal education addresses the whole of life; its understandings, skills, and value development bear on a wide range of occupations and equip one for a lifetime of career mobility. My thesis in this chapter is that liberal education *is* good career preparation.

Too often we regard someone's career as a job held for a long time, and confine "vocation" to the particular work one does, so that anything else becomes avocational and relatively unimportant. But in modern society a lifetime career may involve a wide variety of jobs, different kinds of work with markedly different responsibilities. Career mobility is the key. Moreover in Christian perspective one's vocation in life, while certainly including the work for which she gets paid, is far larger than that work alone. Liberal arts education is the education of responsible agents for the vocation of life itself, life in all its parts and as a whole, which includes the career mobility of one's entire lifetime. So-called vocational training emphasizes particular job information and skills one needs at work. Career preparation requires larger understandings, more transferable skills, richer personal qualities, and some lasting values. This is why I claim that liberal arts education is good career preparation.

To educate people as responsible agents requires attention to their thinking and their values. Of first importance to any employer should be the applicant's *attitude toward work* itself. Among the Greeks an aristocratic attitude prevailed, looking on much of work as debased, as servility, tasks not worthy of the rational, the rich, or the powerful. Our modern economy suggests work is the chore of earning a living by filling a slot that anyone else could fill just as well, or perhaps a rat race to fulfilment and success by climbing the corporate ladder. I would expect the Christian college to help its students see how hollow, how unethical, how unbiblical are those attitudes and the conceptions on which they depend. I would expect students to catch the vision of work as stewardship of God's creation in service to others. The academic dean of one Christian college has in fact claimed that a primary goal of education should be an understanding of the meaning of work in God's economy.[1]

---

1. Joyce Q. Erickson, "Career Education in a Christian Liberal Arts Setting," *Christian Scholars' Review* 6 (1976): 167-79.

This kind of understanding requires *breadth of education*, and that is a second contribution of liberal arts to career preparation. The meaning of work is not a function of management theory or salesmanship. It is rather something we bring *to* management and sales. It draws on psychology and sociology and more basically on the foundational disciplines of theology and philosophy. That kind of breadth is invaluable. The dean of a large university's school of business, for example, suggests five broad areas that are fundamental to business education: psychology, sociology, economics, and mathematics underly our understanding of management processes; historical perspective on our sociopolitical institutions and values is a precondition to understanding labor unions, free enterprise, and alternative economic structures; cross-cultural awareness and foreign area–studies are essential in firms that have international relationships; the humanities, especially literature and philosophy, demand the clear thinking, precise writing, and scrutiny of one's own values that prepare one for any career requiring careful communication and continued self-examination; and the broadly integrative character of liberal learning moves the student beyond narrowly focused analytic techniques to see the overall picture.[2]

Similar prescriptions could be written for other occupations. If human wellness is affected by both environment and the inner life, then the physician will benefit from psychology, sociology, and literature. Increasingly the medical profession faces complex ethical questions on which past practices and existing legislation are silent, questions that call for sound theological principles and the kinds of moral reflection that philosophy practices. The elementary teacher's methods will draw on what he understands of psychology, of family and community structures, and of learning theory. He needs to know what makes good art and good literature good. The minister and missionary need a great deal more than a knowledge of Scripture, the habit of prayer, and a way with people and words: they need an understanding of human beings and

---

2. Joseph A. Pichler, "Ibsen and the Business Schools," *The Chronicle of Higher Education*, Sept. 16, 1977, p. 32.

cultures and socioeconomic problems that is enriched by the social sciences and humanities, and the kind of insight philosophy can give into beliefs other than their own.

After twenty-seven years in prison, Albert Speer, Hitler's minister of munitions, is reported to have said that people who ask what practical purpose there is in studying subjects like history and philosophy need to be reminded that it is only here that fundamental questions are asked—what is a person, what is a good society, what are the proper ends of civilization, and so on. German education, marked by specialization and technical skills, had amassed knowledge without adequate foundations.

Of course, occupational know-how and decision making are more than a matter of background understanding and factual information. *Cognitive and communication skills* are also needful. Words are like clothes, to cover the affront of bare truth and make it presentable. They can either blur its meaning and diffuse its impact, or make it register where it is most needed—whether the words are in business reports, sermons and speeches, or just in ordinary conversation. Style in language like style in clothes carries its own message. Imaginative expression will captivate an audience. Coming directly to the point can crack open the densest material. Many employers tend to put more faith in the applicant's ability to think and communicate than in his college major.

Yet knowledge and cognitive skills are not necessarily enough. One needs as well the *imagination* to come at things in fresh ways, the foresight to come up with alternative game plans, the wisdom to weigh alternatives and make decisions, the persistence that sticks at a task combined with the capacity to change, cooperation combined with independence of mind. These too are traits encouraged by breadth of learning and by liberal education's emphasis on teaching people to think for themselves. The graduate is unlikely to function like a mindless cog in a well-oiled wheel: if that is what an employer wants, she should look elsewhere. But if she wants a thinking, articulate, resourceful young associate with personal integrity, then the Christian liberal arts college is a good place to look. Liberal education is good career preparation.

*Value development* in the Christian college is a career resource that must not be underrated. The fear of the Lord is still the beginning of the moral wisdom society needs. Ethical issues receive increased attention nowadays in both business and the professions, and this is a direction to which the Christian college graduate can significantly contribute. Not that she will always go with the tide. The educated Christian should approach life as a reformer, not just standing around wringing her hands in dismay, nor marching out in disgust to set up a separate Christian enclave, but working within the structure of things to change it for the better. She has learned that justice and compassion, the makings of social righteousness, belong in the work place where she stands as a representative of God's kingdom.

The same understandings, skills, and values that constitute good career preparation make good life preparation as well. Family life, friendships, community service, church involvements, and the use of leisure—all stand to benefit in analogous fashion from an education that is broad enough to help people understand the purposes and functioning of those things, and develop appropriate interests and skills. The need for Christian businesspeople who will struggle to apply Christian ethics in their marketing programs and personnel policies is matched by the need for Christian marriages, Christian parents and friends, Christian artists, Christian public servants, Christian professionals—and for Christian churches that will support them and their colleges because they too see life whole as a calling from God.

The potential of Christian higher education is inspiring. I dream about Christian college students and their future roles in life. I dream of those who go on to graduate school to teach at the college level, and I see them as a generation of Christian scholars and teachers strategically located in the colleges and universities of this and other lands, penetrating the thought-patterns of their culture with Christian beliefs and values. I dream of those who go into law and medicine, into

business and education, into the armed forces, into govern-
ment, into marriage, and I envision their influence in reviving
the Christian foundations of Western society. I dream of those
who go on to seminary to preach and teach the Word of God
and I pray that they may bring to the church a new sense of
relevance. I look for the voice of the prophet, speaking from
the evangelical pulpit about the sins of society: economic injustice, violence and sexual license, self-indulgent affluence,
power struggles in politics, education, and business. I look for
the prophet calling men and women to turn repentingly to
God, to practice justice and compassion not only in this land
but among all the nations of the earth. I dream of the massive
impact for truth and righteousness that God can make both
here and for eternity through them, with their educational
opportunities.

The value of liberal education as career preparation
does not depend on how many "vocational" courses we load
into the curriculum. It may in fact depend on limiting the
number of "vocational" hours credited toward a degree. With
good reason a recent study of public education called for grade-
school teachers to major in one of the traditional disciplines
rather than in teacher education as such.

Three things should be kept in mind. First, vocational
courses are usually available to students in the summer or on
a semester off. The Christian liberal arts college does not have
to satisfy every such desire, and perhaps should devote its
resources to what is more central to the strategy of integrated
Christian liberal learning.

Second, in our highly specialized and technological
society, most college graduates will need further schooling as
career directions take shape, be it in medical or law school or
an MBA program or seminary. In this sense, the liberal arts
college provides precareer education.

Third, the undergraduate college builds bridges toward various kinds of occupations in a variety of ways. Courses
like urban sociology, medical or business ethics, and philosophy of law are obviously related. Visiting speakers provide
a constant flow of role models and resource people. Internships

help the student to experience what an occupation is like—perhaps to discover what she does *not* want to do—and they enrich an education if they require disciplinary input and careful examination of methodology, theoretical assumptions, and the ethical issues encountered. Departments advise about career possibilities and graduate programs that lead in those directions. But much of the onus falls on the college's placement office or career center, both for "selling" its liberal arts graduates to unenlightened employers and for educating students about the job search: identifying aptitudes and interests, gaining job-related experience, preparing a vita, interviewing, and the rest. With this kind of assistance liberal education is indeed good career preparation.

# 5 INTEGRATING FAITH AND LEARNING

It is not sufficient for a Christian college to identify itself simply as a liberal arts institution; it is also an extended arm of the church. We have laid aside various inadequate attempts to justify the combination. A Christian college does not exist to combine good education with a protective atmosphere, for Christians believe that the source of evil is ultimately within the heart, not without. The Christian college does not exist only to offer biblical and theological studies, for these are available in other kinds of institutions, and could be offered through adjunct programs at state universities without the tremendous expense of offerings in the arts and sciences. The distinctive of the Christian college is not that it cultivates piety and religious commitment, for this could be done by church-sponsored residence houses on secular campuses. Rather the Christian college is distinctive in that the Christian faith can touch the entire range of life and learning to which a liberal education exposes students.

In principle Christian perspectives are all-redeeming and all-transforming, and it is this which gives rise to the idea of integrating faith with learning. I say "in principle" because often in practice faith and learning interact rather than integrate. Integration is an ideal never fully accomplished by anyone but God himself. Public relations material sometimes states that faith and learning are integrated on campus, as if a stroke of the pen makes it an accomplished fact, but there is many a miss and fumble and bungle between the purpose and the achievement. Interaction differs from integration. In interaction the two sit side by side in real contact with each other and engage in dialog on a variety of particulars. Yet we need more than this if we are going to relate faith and learning as a coherent whole from the ground up.

Sometimes even interaction has been repressed in favor of indoctrination, as if prepackaged answers can satisfy inquiring minds. Students need rather to gain a realistic look at life and to discover for themselves the questions that confront us. They need to work their way painfully through the maze of alternative ideas and arguments while finding out how the Christian faith speaks to such matters. They need a teacher as a catalyst and guide, one who has struggled and is struggling with similar questions and knows some of the pertinent materials and procedures. They need to be exposed to the frontiers of learning where problems are still not fully formulated and knowledge is exploding, and where by the very nature of things indoctrination is impossible.

Sometimes interaction between faith and learning has been at little more than a defensive level, an apologetic against challenges to the faith from the world of thought, or a Christian critique of its competitors. Apologetics undoubtedly has a place, but the Christian college has a larger and more constructive job than this. Integration is concerned not so much with attack and defense as with the positive contributions of human learning to an understanding of the faith and to the development of a Christian worldview, and with the positive contribution of the Christian faith to all the arts and sciences. Certainly learning has contributed from all fields to the church's understanding and propagation of its faith, from the early church to the present day, and the Christian college can contribute signally in that way. But it must also grasp what is not as often recognized, that faith affects learning far more deeply than learning affects faith.

Integration should be seen not as an achievement or a position but as an intellectual activity that goes on as long as we keep learning anything at all. Not only as an intellectual activity, however, for integrated learning will contribute to the integration of faith into every dimension of a person's life and character.

In what follows, I shall propose four approaches to the integration of faith and learning.

## THE ATTITUDINAL APPROACH

There are some areas in higher education where Christianity seems at first glance to make no evident difference. Performance fields are a prime example: the vocalist, the pianist, the sculptor, or the gymnast, even the research chemist or the mathematician. It hardly makes sense to speak of "Christian piano" or "Christian gymnastics." Admittedly, the Dutch philosopher Herman Dooyeweerd refers to "Christian mathematics": yet he is thinking not of proofs and procedures but rather of the foundations of mathematics and the fact that God and the law-governed nature of his creation make mathematics possible at all.

Especially in performance areas and in the disciplined development of skills (although certainly not only there), the attitude of the teacher or student is the initial and perhaps most salient point of contact with the Christian faith. If I were teaching symbolic logic, which is as close as a philosopher comes to mathematics, my Christianity would come through in my attitude and my intellectual integrity far more than in the actual content of the course. A positive, inquiring attitude and a persistent discipline of time and ability express the value I find in learning because of my theology and my Christian commitment.

A positive attitude toward liberal learning is not always evident among Christians. From time to time in the history of the church as in history generally, a kind of anti-intellectualism or a cultural escapism has erupted. But the Christian faith rightly understood creates a positive attitude toward liberal learning because in God's creation every area of life and learning is related to the wisdom and power of God. All truth is God's truth.

The same positive attitude affects more than the pursuit of truth. In his famous *City of God* Augustine proposes

48

a Christian conception of a just society in place of Cicero's pagan view: justice is giving to each his due, including God, and that ability, like every good and perfect gift, comes from God. It therefore takes reverence and love for God to motivate us adequately toward justice. The same attitude should affect aesthetic values like beauty and creativity. All beauty is from God no matter where it is found, the artistic creativity of people is God's good gift, the potential of physical materials for being formed and fashioned into objects of art is God's doing. Some writers have even developed an aesthetic argument for the existence of God, based on the correlation between human creativity in the arts and the adaptability of the world to this creativity. In God's creation every area of the liberal arts has to do with God.

Elton Trueblood has said that the Christian scholar is likely to be a better scholar for being a Christian than one would be otherwise. The comparison is not between the Christian and the non-Christian scholar, because there are other variables involved when you compare two people, but between the one individual as Christian and the same person as non-Christian. The reason, says Trueblood, is motivation, for the Christian faith is the sworn enemy of all intellectual dishonesty and shoddiness.[1] The Christian believes that in all that she does intellectually, socially, or artistically, she is handling God's creation and that is sacred.

Shortly after World War II Arnold Nash wrote that one of the main tasks of the Christian scholar in higher education is to discover the meaning of Christian vocation.[2] I submit that a genuinely Christian attitude finds meaning in the vocation of a chemist or a sociologist, a historian or a psychologist, a mathematician or an artist. The scholar's love of truth becomes an expression of love for God, just as the citizen's love of justice in society can be an expression of hunger and thirst for righteousness, and the artist's love for the creative and the beautiful expresses love for the Creator.

1. *The Idea of a College* (Harper, 1959), p. 19.
2. *The University and the Modern World* (Macmillan, 1944), p. 292.

This is where the Christian college student must begin. The first task of integration is at the personal level of attitude and motivation. In an overtly Christian college, Christian teachers dealing with Christian students have a point of appeal that is not available elsewhere. Admittedly, motivating students is difficult. Adolescents have a tendency to intellectual sloppiness and their characteristic self-interestedness comes out as much in the life of the mind as anywhere. Enthusiasm for liberal learning often runs against the peer-group attitude that general education is a necessary evil to be gotten out of the way as soon and as painlessly as possible, rather than an alluring window on God's creation. It also runs against the suspicion with which many have been taught to regard the intellect and imagination, and against their cultural isolation. Yet if our highest end is to glorify God and to enjoy him forever, we must pursue this end here and now by exploring and enjoying the richness of his creation, and we can do so in Christian liberal arts education.

Somehow or other the student must realize that education is a Christian vocation, one's prime calling from God for these years, that education must be an act of love, of worship, of stewardship, a wholehearted response to God. Attitude and motivation accordingly afford but a beginning; this personal contact between faith and learning should extend to disciplined scholarship and to intellectual and artistic integrity.

The college must therefore cultivate an atmosphere of Christian learning, a level of eager expectancy that is picked up by anyone who is on campus for even a short while. It must sell the idea from the point of student recruitment and admission through freshman orientation into the residence hall program, the curriculum and individual courses. The chapel program must exemplify this attitude rather than the unthinking disjuction that is all too frequent between faith and devotion on the one hand and what goes on in the classroom on the other. In campus publications, in the counseling program, a perennial salesman's job has to be done on the idea that liberal education is the Christian vocation of students as well as teachers. And required general education courses must present not narrow specializations in isolation from each other, but ideas that stretch the mind, open up historical perspective, enlarge windows on the world, and reveal the creative impact of Christian faith and thought.

The most important single factor in the teacher is the attitude toward learning. By virtue of what a teacher is, his students can stand on his shoulders and peer further in their day than he did in his. From the teacher the alluring contours of a Christian mind begin to emerge.

## THE ETHICAL APPROACH

Ethical issues arise in the college admissions process, in matters of equal opportunity, and in distributing financial aid. They arise in how we approach learning, in the use of materials, of research methods, and of computers, in experiments involving human subjects, in respecting copyrights and crediting other peoples' work. (Plagiarism is perhaps the college student's most common form of stealing, akin to the commercial espionage that steals crucial information by sifting through a competitor's garbage.) Ethical issues also arise in the uses society makes of its knowledge, in what we do or do not do to our environment and with nonrenewable resources, in genetic research and over nuclear wastes, with management techniques and manipulative advertising, in economic policy and international politics. Questions of justice and mercy haunt us continually, calling for active integration of factual understanding with moral values rooted in the Christian faith.

For some years we heard talk of value-neutral education and of value-free science. The underlying assumption is that we live in a world of bare facts, that empirical knowledge bears no intrinsic relation (only a coincidental one) to moral or social values, and that value judgments are purely relative expressions of subjective feelings and conventional attitudes. Facts are value-neutral; education and science are concerned with facts, not feelings.

While these positivist assumptions are extremely

doubtful on both philosophical and theological grounds, the education of responsible agents in any case requires attention to values and value judgments. World War II, Hiroshima, and the Holocaust awakened many Western educators to this, and especially since Vietnam and the activist '60s it is virtually impossible to keep social issues and value judgments out of the classroom—even where relativist and subjectivist ethical theories still prevail. Indeed, language itself is so value-laden as to render value-neutrality almost impossible. Growing up in England I was introduced to the American Revolution by a *footnote* to colonial history about the *revolt* of the American colonies. Word choice and the organization of material gave the game away.

Language is loaded in other ways too, so that it is not enough to label things "right" or "wrong," "just" or "loving." The word "love," for example, is used promiscuously today, but it means something different in a Christian context than in pop psychology and most popular lyrics. Confused values often ride piggyback on identical terms. We must sort them out and be clear about what we mean to say, what others mean too.

In teaching, value judgments should not be moralizing tacked on at the end of a supposedly factual recital, nor should they be pontificated. Rather an evaluative process can run through the structure of a course, in the selection of topics, in the assumptions stated at the outset, in assigned readings and papers. It may be true that a social science does not as such make Christian value judgments, but the Christian social scientist is still not a schizophrenic. If she is a Christian, her values will somehow or other show themselves, consciously or unconsciously, in her work. It had better be conscious and well reasoned rather than unconscious and unreasoned, or else it will likely appear dishonest and be confused.

The ethical approach to integration, in other words, must explore the intrinsic relationship between the facts and the values of justice and love, a relationship that goes beyond the question of consequences. The key to the fact-value relationship lies rather in what ethicists call "middle-level concepts." Relating the factual circumstances of a business to ethical questions about wages and prices is the middle-level concept of work, its meaning and its purposes. Relating facts about crime to questions about sentencing is the middle-level concept of punishment and it purposes. Relating the facts about Richard and Mary, their feelings for one another, to the obvious question they are facing is the middle-level concept of marriage, its meaning and its purpose. The ethical approach must focus on the meaning of and God's purpose for work, punishment, and marriage, drawing on both biblical teaching and theological reflection related to these particular areas.

Middle-level concepts are necessary but not sufficient. We must also be clear about the overall biblical principles of justice and love. In addressing ethical issues, three questions are essential if we are to integrate Christian principles into ethical discussion.

1. What are the facts in the case, including contributing causes and possible consequences? Here the relevant sciences are important.

2. What middle-level concepts are involved? What are the purposes God intended for this area of human activity? Here theology and philosophy come into play.

3. What policy or action is called for in this kind of case or situation? How can we pursue proper purposes with justice and with love for all those involved? Here all the above considerations and disciplines come into play.[3]

### THE FOUNDATIONAL APPROACH

Both the attitudinal and the ethical approaches uncover various assumptions with which Christians and others approach learning. The assumptions are part of the history of ideas, and particularly in the West that history shows the interplay of conflicting theological and philosophical traditions. This is true in every area of learning, for each of them has

---

3. See further my *Ethics: Approaching Moral Decisions* (Inter-Varsity Press, 1984), chaps. 6-8.

historical and philosophical foundations. "Foundations of Mathematics" and "Foundations of Education" are even common course titles. Curriculum studies in a number of major universities identify history and philosophy as "foundational disciplines," and in Christian colleges theology becomes a third foundational area. These three are the focus of a "foundational" approach to integration.[4]

History is strategic in this regard when it is studied not just as a factual chronicle of rulers and wars and dates, but more as cultural and intellectual history. In that perspective it reveals the significance of ideas and values out of which people (reflective and valuing agents, that is) have acted. It becomes a history of governing ideals, and it includes the creative and redemptive influence of Christianity in the shaping of our culture.

What, for instance, about the origins of modern science? The philosopher and scientist A. N. Whitehead suggests that early modern science developed because of the encouragement given to it in the religious atmosphere of the Middle Ages. This thesis has been challenged, but if it is not overstated I think it can be substantiated. The atmosphere of the Middle Ages was pervaded by the theistic conviction that because God is the rational and wise Creator, his handiwork is therefore intelligible to beings in God's image. This theistic atmosphere which expected the natural order to be amenable to rational inquiry was the natural birthplace of scientific inquiry. Fifty years ago, the British philosopher Michael Foster published a series of articles arguing that the Greek conception that eternal forms determine the course of nature led the ancients to rationalistic speculations rather than to empirical observation, until the theistic insistence prevailed in science as in theology that nature is contingent on God. There is no intrinsic necessity that it exist or that it be the way it is. If it is God's creation, it is contingent on God, and the scientist can no longer operate on an a priori basis but must be more

---

4. See chap. 1, note 4. Also Nicholas Wolterstorff, *Reason within the Bounds of Religion* (Eerdmans, 1976).

empirical if he is to find out how nature does in fact behave. The result, according to Foster, was the growth of Renaissance science.[5]

The historical approach has considerable merit in the humanities. In introducing students to philosophy, one obvious way to expose the effect of Christian perspectives is to include readings from first-rate philosophers of the past who were themselves Christian theists. That is usually far more effective than a teacher's own half-baked, underdeveloped notions. One might include Christian philosophers of different sorts: Augustine's Christianization of Cicero; Aquinas's use of Aristotelian ideas; Descartes, Leibniz, Locke, and Berkeley and their attempts to justify and limit human reason in dependence on God, while avoiding dangers inherent in the current mechanistic view of nature and of man; Kierkegaard's criticism of Enlightenment epistemology and ethics. Christian philosophers as different as these reflect the pluralism within a Christian worldview, yet they share the common belief that God created all things and that man is uniquely in God's image, and they develop the creative impact of these ideas on the problems they wrestled with and in the positions they set forth.

Be it the history of science or of philosophy or of art or whatever, we have available historical samples of faith in creative contact with learning. They give us precedents on which to build, a tradition in which we too stand. They underscore the fact that God is at work in the history of the arts and sciences, as well as in the church and the nations, and this history continues today in our own efforts at a constructive relation of faith and learning.

Philosophical foundations are every bit as important, whether they be in philosophy of science, or philosophical psychology, or aesthetic and critical theory, or whatever. What one assumes about the nature and limitations of scientific explanation affects not only what explanations are proposed and

---

5. A. N. Whitehead, *Science and the Modern World* (Mentor Books, 1948), p. 14; M. B. Foster in *Mind* 43 (1934): 446; 44 (1935): 439; 45 (1936): 1.

how they will be evaluated, but also whether other kinds of explanation (religious ones for example) are to be accepted. Theories of literary criticism in similar fashion determine what sort of meaning a piece may have, indeed for Derrida and the deconstructionists whether it can have any public meaning at all. Philosophies of history, and theories of human personality underlying them, speak to questions of historical causation: the Marxist, the Freudian, and the Christian therefore read history quite differently, as they do sociology and literature and everything else. Philosophical foundations concern methods of knowing and interpreting (epistemology), conceptions of reality (metaphysics), and basic values. Every discipline has such foundations, and they are utterly strategic for Christian integration. Disagreements about other particular interpretations and theories are often rooted here.

This is partly why theological foundations are essential too, for Christian theology has philosophical implications. The Christian revelation claim puts limitations on the scope of scientific knowledge. Its understanding of the human person runs counter to much in Marxist and other forms of naturalistic thinking. One must be alert to such tensions—as well as to commonalities—if one is to think with integrity as a Christian. By the same token, theological foundations should underly a Christian ethic, a theory of social change, an aesthetic—not that they answer all the philosophical questions, but rather that they point constructive directions on foundational issues. The Christian in philosophy needs to be theologically informed, if integration is to proceed, but by the same token the theologian must be philosophically informed if he is to contribute to foundational thinking. In fact an entire Christian college faculty might fruitfully work through the major topics of systematic theology, asking how each topic touches the foundations of its disciplines.

The greatest effect of Christian theology is undoubtedly in the humanities, because there we find explicit views of human nature, of God, of morals, and of life. Yet paradoxically Christians have frequently exhibited least interest here. The next greatest influence is in the social and behavioral sciences, where the concern is with human behavior and institutions. The least far-ranging impact of Christian theology is in the natural sciences, despite the fact that more has probably been written about the relationship of Christianity to science than to other areas. Evangelicals have stressed the "how" of creation, yet the biblical teaching has more far-reaching essentials—one is in the essential character of theism as against Gnostic dualism and pantheism and naturalism. As Langdon Gilkey well shows in his *Maker of Heaven and Earth*, creation *ex nihilo* speaks to the problems of good and evil, freedom and individuality, and meaning in life. Another essential is the uniqueness of people in the image of God. The effect of these items on the content of natural science is much less than their effect in the social sciences and humanities. In addition, the doctrines of sin and grace, biblical conceptions of history and of social justice, and the whole range of doctrines need exploring.

Unfortunately the gaps between our disciplines too often prevent the benefits of interdepartmental interaction. The scientist or literature teacher can come out of the best graduate school with little more than an eighth-grade theology, and perhaps less philosophy. Too often the psychologist is unacquainted with the philosophical limitations of empirical methods or with recent philosophical work on the nature of mind. And the sociologist is often a stranger to ethical theory and so a novice at arguing on other than dogmatic or utilitarian grounds, or is unacquainted with Old Testament social ethics. Nor do philosophers and theologians necessarily help. Too many of them are content to insulate themselves within their analyses and exegeses, rather than interacting with the arts and sciences their work should affect.

Somehow this syndrome must be broken. Interdisciplinary courses are premature before the teachers involved know enough about each others' fields to construct and conduct a unified course. Time must first be found for interdisciplinary dialog among faculty. Meanwhile it would help if every student were required to take not only a course in Christian theology and a general introduction to philosophy that stresses the nature of philosophical inquiry and selects from the heritage of Western thought, but also a course that bridges either outward from another discipline toward religion and philosophy or inward from philosophy to another discipline. Philosophy of science or of mind, social ethics or aesthetics, philosophy of history or religion, of politics or law—these are the courses that address the foundational questions with which other disciplines contact philosophy. At least a requirement in these areas would help the next generation of college teachers to do what the present generation has not always been able to accomplish in interpreting scientific and scholarly findings.

## THE WORLDVIEW APPROACH

The most embracing contact between Christianity and human learning is the all-encompassing world and life view. The Christian faith enables us to see all things in relationship to God as their Creator, Redeemer, and Lord, and from this central focus an integrating worldview emerges. The contemporary university tends to concentrate on the parts rather than the whole and to come away with a fragmented view of life that lacks overall meaning. Arnold Nash calls this tendency "intellectual polytheism,"[6] to underscore that it is as much a commitment to a worldview as is Christian theism. The influence of intellectual polytheism has been calamitous. When a multitude of studies is conducted with no interrelationships the university becomes a multiversity. In theory the university rejects attempts to teach any one conception of the world but in practice it teaches a fragmented view of life. Even to take a "neutral" position is to take some position. The worldview-ish issues cannot be avoided.

More recently Robert Brombaugh, professor of philosophy at Yale University, stated in his Presidential Address to the Metaphysical Society of America,

We are doing an increasingly brisk and precise job in secondary school science in demonstrating the case for a world of fact that

---

6. *The University and the Modern World*, pp. 258ff.

admits no glimmer of caprice, freedom, or change in its causal order. We are doing an increasingly more crucial job of awakening a sense of responsibility in our students. Sometimes they feel this responsibility toward society, sometimes toward their own authenticity. But we are doing nothing at all to explain this schizophrenic change in the conception of reality that varies with each move between classrooms. We are upset by the attempts of our students to retain some intellectual integrity: by apathy, by indiscriminate activism, by distrust of an intelligence and authority that has set them a puzzle they must solve, with pieces that cannot be fitted together into any solution.[7]

It is a sad paradox that on the one hand the scientific outlook declares that nature is intelligible and rationally ordered in both its macroscopic and its microscopic aspects, and on the other hand the pessimist tells us that life is devoid of any intrinsic meaning and intelligible order at all. Ours is a schizophrenic day that desperately needs an integrated understanding, a worldview that can stick fragmented pieces together. The Christian is obliged to develop a Christian worldview, believing as he does that the Christian message heals.

But what do we mean by a worldview, a *Weltanschauung?* The notion needs unpacking, and I suggest four characteristics.[8]

The first and most obvious is that a worldview is holistic or integrational. It sees things not just as parts but also as a whole. It is a systematic understanding and appraisal of life, and none of the academic disciplines is exempted from contact with it.

Second, a worldview is exploratory, not a closed system worked out once and for all but an endless undertaking that is still but the vision of a possibility, an unfinished symphony barely begun. It explores the creative and redemptive impact of the Christian revelation on every dimension of thought and life, and it remains open-ended because the task is so vast

---

7. "Applied Metaphysics: Truth and Passing Time," *Review of Metaphysics* 19 (1966): 650-51.

8. For a fuller statement see my *Contours of a World View* (Eerdmans, 1983).

that to complete it would require the omniscience of God. To begin requires an intelligent understanding of the Christian revelation, and from this first glimpse of truth as a whole endless inquiry grows. We should not expect the Christian college to propound a definite and complete Christian view of things, for it is premature to finalize all the details of a Christian view of this, that or anything. Christian perspectives are possible, but not a complete and definitive system. Who are we bungling, stuttering creatures to exhaust any subject? Now we see through a glass darkly; we know in part.

Third, a Christian worldview is likely to be pluralistic. If it is an open-ended exploration you cannot expect complete unanimity—not that there is much virtue in human unanimity anyway. Even within a particular Christian tradition, say the Reformed, there should be room for pluralism in the development of various perspectives each equally loyal to Reformed theology. Historic Christianity taken as a whole has been even more pluralistic. Diversity exists not only because of theological difference but also because we explore Christian perspectives on the world of thought at different points and by different paths and with different concerns and backgrounds. This is why academic freedom and intellectual honesty are so essential.

Fourth, a worldview is confessional and perspectival. We need not proceed deductively from universal and necessary truths, from either axioms or scientifically demonstrable propositions, so I prefer not to call the starting point "presuppositions." Rather we start with a confession of faith, with an admixture of beliefs and attitudes and values. Good and sufficient reason may be given for what we believe, but ours is still a confessional stance and from the perspective of this confession we look at life. We see things from a Christian point of view.

A world and life view is not the same as a theology: Christian theology is a study of the perspective itself as disclosed by the biblical revelation. It looks within, whereas a Christian worldview looks without, at life and thought in other departments and disciplines, in order to see these other things from the standpoint of revelation and as an interrelated whole.

Integration is ultimately concerned to see things whole from a Christian perspective, to penetrate thought with that perspective, to think Christianly.

The four characteristics of a worldview, then, are that it is (1) holistic, (2) exploratory, (3) pluralistic, and (4) perspectival, and the four approaches I have suggested to integration are (1) the attitudinal, (2) the ethical, (3) the foundational, and (4) the worldviewish.

# 6 ACADEMIC FREEDOM

On the surface at least, the Christian liberal arts college faces a dilemma. On the one hand, liberal education requires that we think critically about our heritage of faith and culture and wrestle honestly with the problems humankind in general and Christians in particular face in today's world. This requires freedom of inquiry for both teacher and student. On the other hand, Christian education implies commitment to the Word of God and responsibility to the church constituency a college serves. Liberty without loyalty is not Christian, but loyalty without the liberty to think for oneself is not education.

It is also true that education is impossible without loyalty to truth and intellectual honesty, and that a person without loyalties outside himself has not yet joined the human race; likewise that loyalty without liberty is not Christian but legalistic. The attempt to integrate faith and learning and to see things from a confessional perspective is, after all, an attempt to unite loyalty with liberty in Christian education.

In this chapter I want to discuss (1) why academic freedom is important in the Christian college, (2) how it may be conceived, and (3) some criticisms it meets.

## IMPORTANCE

Academic freedom is essential to the academic task. Liberal education means the stretching of minds and imaginations, the unceasing stimulus to honest inquiry, the appropriation of a cultural heritage, the transmission of ideas and values, an exposure to the frontiers of learning. By definition it requires freedom to grow, to gain stimulation and to give it, freedom to meet great minds of the past and present, to interact rigorously with their ideas and weigh their values, freedom to explore new horizons and press back the frontiers of learning—in a word, it means academic freedom.

The Germans had two words: *Lehrfreiheit,* the freedom to teach, and *Lernfreiheit,* the freedom to learn. The sort of neutrality they intended by these terms may be undesirable for both educational and religious reasons and impossible psychologically. But they serve to point up two sides to academic freedom: the faculty side and the student side. Both are of concern in liberal education, and together they amount to the freedom of a college really to be an educational institution rather than an indoctrination center or a political tool.

Further, academic freedom is essential for theological reasons. A person is not an automaton but a free agent created in God's image. If we produce stereotypes cut from the same pattern, if we repress individuality, we sin against both God and society, for individuals do not exist for individualism's sake but to live in communion with God and community with their fellows.

But freedom is essential to faith. Freedom of thought is the freedom to think for oneself with the faith one has and the beliefs and values to which one is committed. In this sense neither faith nor intellect can be forced but must be free, full, and wholehearted, or else one does not really believe and does not think. Richard Hofstadter observes that in the Reformation period, "pious men saw that forced acceptance of a faith would not be sincere, that instead of saving souls it created hypocrites."[1]

Academic freedom is the recognition that faith and intellect, like love, cannot be forced and must not be, if each is to play its part in relation to the other. I suspect that a considerable amount of student cynicism and skepticism can

---

1. R. Hofstadter and W. P. Metzger, *The Development of Academic Freedom in the United States* (Columbia University Press, 1955), p. 65.

be traced to attempts to impose a faith dogmatically rather than presenting it graciously and reasonably, and to the practice of pontificating "answers" rather than assisting students in grappling with issues for themselves in the light of their heritage of Christian faith and thought. We can get so busy taking the motes of immaturity out of students' eyes that we forget the beams of finiteness, fallibility, and inflexibility in our own eyes.

While Scripture is our final rule of faith and practice, not all the truth about everything is fully revealed therein. If that were so we would need no natural or social sciences, no humanities and no theology—just biblical exegesis. Rather, the eternal Logos has left his imprint on nature and human beings and history, and the truth discovered therein is God's truth too. We approach it with reverence and humility, modest and tentative in our pronouncements. If all truth is God's truth, we must be free to explore it. If it all ultimately fits into a coherent whole, then our task is to interpret it as such by developing Christian perspectives in the natural and social sciences and the humanities, so as to structure a Christian worldview that exhibits plainly the principle that truth is one and all truth is God's. This requires open eyes and open doors on the world, not blinkers and cloisters and defensiveness about the problem.

The fact is that faith liberates rather than enslaves the mind. It helps me understand myself and my world, it creates a positive attitude toward learning. Christian liberty is neither irresponsible license nor repressive bondage, and academic freedom in the Christian college must rest on this realization.

According to Russell Kirk, the medieval universities enjoyed academic freedom not despite but because of the framework of Christian belief in which they operated. Insofar as their scholars were Christian, this framework did not restrain them. Rather it protected their dialog, it guaranteed them liberty to pursue the truth in detail and in totality and to lead their students into the same enterprise of committed scholarship.

The teacher was a servant of God wholly, and of God only. His freedom was sanctioned by an authority more than human. Now and then that freedom was violated . . . yet it scarcely occurred to anyone to attempt to regulate or to suppress the freedom of the Academic: it was regarded almost as a part of the natural and unalterable order of things. In medieval times, it was precisely their Christian framework that gave masters and students this high confidence. Far from repressing free discussion, this framework encouraged disputation of a heated intensity almost unknown in universities nowadays. . . . They were free from a stifling internal conformity, because the whole purpose of the universities was the search after an enduring truth, beside which worldly aggrandizement was as nothing. They were free because they agreed on this one thing, if on nothing else, that the fear of God is the beginning of wisdom.[2]

Finally, academic freedom is essential to the self-scrutiny and improvement of any society. Socrates and Plato are classic examples in their struggle with the Sophists for the survival of Athenian culture. As we read Plato's dialogs, we recognize with a smile that portrait of the teacher as a skillful midwife and the experience of students who feel the birth-pangs that climax intellectual gestation. As we survey Plato's own intellectual development and examine the educational philosophy and program he presents in the *Republic,* we are impressed with his concern for society, with his emphasis on unchanging values, with his integration of the curriculum around the disciplined mind, with his emphasis on critical thinking. We note the diversity of viewpoints discussed, the lack not only of unanimity but also of dogmatic indoctrination. Admittedly he censored some of the literature of his day because it detracted from intellectual and moral growth. But we admire his relentless quest for clarity of understanding, his endless self-scrutiny, and the courageous intellectual honesty that led Socrates to lose his life and forced Plato to change his mind. The Socratic method presupposes freedom to pursue the truth even in a community that is unaccustomed to thinking

---

2. Russell Kirk, *Academic Freedom* (Regnery, 1955), p. 18.

and unfavorably disposed to penetrating inquiry. Socrates embarrassed and antagonized his constituencies, perhaps unnecessarily; he was accused of corrupting his students, the youth of Athens, in the final analysis because his supreme loyalty was to eternal truth rather than human opinion, and this loyalty could not be swayed by the fears and psychological insecurities of others, and would not be trampled by political pressure. His motivation was not that of the Sophist libertines, but that of a loyal and responsible citizen, utterly convinced that what he did was for the common good and in the highest interests of society.

The point is that liberal education and the freedom it requires can provide the basis for an informed and responsible criticism of society. If colleges are to provide leadership, then embryonic leaders must try their wings even if first attempts fail. What better way is there to criticize and improve on the past and present than to examine it in the light of the best learning available? How else can we who are historical beings hope to transcend the past more creatively in the future?

It is likewise important to the ongoing history of the church, for its vigor in meeting new challenges and its creativity in relating unchanging truth to changing situations, that it expose itself to possible criticism based on responsible learning. It is not by accident that freedom of conscience is part of the Reformation heritage. The early leaders of the Reformation—Wycliffe, Huss and Luther—were university men and their opposition to Rome developed because they refused to think in ruts worn by tradition, superstition, and ignorance. Wycliffe was stoutly defended by Oxford University against pope and bishop, and it took the combined force of church and crown to suppress his voice. Religious liberty and academic freedom went hand in hand, insisting on the right to examine the cherished and to improve on the past. Not only reformers were repressed. Aristotle and Aquinas had been banned at Paris; later, elsewhere, Descartes, Newton, and Locke shared the same fate. And remember Galileo. But truth will win out. It cannot be suppressed; for in the final analysis all truth is God's.

We sadly err if we repeat the errors of the past, whether in excising twentieth-century Aristotles from the curriculum, or in seeking to silence our Galileos or Wycliffes. This is no way to face problems; it is dishonest. There is no effective alternative to academic freedom. The Christian college must provide the opportunity and the atmosphere for an open discussion of new ideas and significant issues. Hackneyed clichés and parroted answers smack more of indoctrination than education. There is no substitute for the hard work of thinking and no escape from the ever present possibility of misunderstanding.

The evangelical theologian G. C. Berkouwer states it plainly:

> An honesty which has a candid eye open to the problems of the day is basically Christian and belongs to our Christian responsibilities. If we were to renege on this Christian responsibility, we would confine Christian life to a ghetto of irrelevancy and powerlessness.[3]

To deny academic freedom is historical suicide. Rather than confirming men in the truth it will drive them from it. Rather than cherishing orthodoxy it will render it suspect to every inquiring mind. Rather than developing the intellectual resources essential to Christian thought and action it will stifle them. Rather than launching a strategic offensive into the citadels of secularism it will incarcerate us in the ill-equipped and outdated strongholds of past wars. The Church Militant cannot retreat; but to advance means facing problems squarely, entertaining new ideas, admitting and correcting mistakes. Truth is not yet fully known; every academic discipline is subject to change, correction, and expansion—even theology. Students must know this and must be taught to think for themselves. On its academic front, then, the effectiveness of the Church Militant requires academic freedom.

The Christian college is a uniquely American institution, and the history of academic freedom within its halls is

---

3. *Christianity Today*, August 2, 1963, p. 48.

therefore a chapter in the history of American Christianity. Of particular importance is the rise of theological liberalism with its repudiation of biblical authority. It is little wonder that as liberal forces engulfed church-related institutions, conservatives became suspicious of the treachery that turns liberty into license. Yet it is unfortunate that in repudiating the one extreme of license, they have sometimes tended to the other extreme of legalism and become suspicious even of that academic integrity and freedom which is an expression of Christian honesty and liberty.

Academic freedom, in other words, is a necessity, not a luxury. It is of the essence both of Christianity and of learning and must be so defined and practiced. It is of the essence of Christianity because true freedom, the liberty we have in Christ, mediates between the extremes of license and legalism. It is of the essence of learning because the true learner is a humble, teachable person, free from the dictatorship of all but the truth.

### DEFINITION

Academic freedom is the freedom of the teacher to teach, of the student to learn, and of the college to be an educational institution. In a Christian college it should exemplify a Christian liberty that avoids the extremes both of legalism and of license. This suggests three possible policies: the legalistic, the libertine, and responsible freedom. Russell Kirk aptly describes them as follows:

> In the eyes of the Indoctrinators, the scholar and teacher are servants, hired for money to do a job. In the eyes of the Doctrinaire Liberals, the scholar and the teacher are masterless men, rather like Cain, and ought to remain so. In my eyes the scholar and the teacher are Bearers of the Word—that is, the conservators and promulgators of knowledge in all its forms; they are neither simply hired functionaries nor simply knights-errant in their lists.[4]

I think of the indoctrinator as the dogmatist for whom

---

4. *Academic Freedom*, p. 31.

all issues are settled and all truth known and, as a result, all creative scholarship erodes away. He is the legalist who, enforcing things as they are, forgets that faith, like love, cannot be forced, but rather rises as a person's free response to the revelation of truth, a response out of an enlightened mind freed from the shackles of opinion and prejudice. The indoctrinator has a ready-made set of answers for every question. But when his students meet new problems or start to think for themselves, they have neither the answers nor the developed intellectual powers to work them out. Having learned neither the meaning nor the use of their freedom, they either remain shackled by fear or else become disillusioned libertines, the campus cynics whose loyalty is to themselves rather than to the God of truth. Christian indoctrination is a self-contradiction for the educator who purports to develop the individuality and intellectual powers of persons created in God's image.

On the other extreme, the "freedom bandwagon" collides head-on with the legitimate concerns of society and its institutions. The libertine interprets "education for democracy" to mean one that ensures absolute equality; no viewpoint can be more true than another: all stand on the same level and are to be presented with a benign and uncritical relativism. His presupposition is that nothing is true in itself; truth is relative, and ideas are but the tools of successful adjustment. He tries to solve problems without any fixed reference in eternal truth and unchanging values.

For those whose ultimate loyalty is to the expedient and the popular rather than to truth, Socrates would have a goading question; so would the medieval scholars, the scholarly victims of Nazi oppression, and our Christian forbears. It is the question of the apostle, "Whether it be right in the sight of God to hearken unto you more than unto God, judge ye. For we cannot but speak the things which we have seen and heard" (Acts 4:19-20, KJV). To the libertine this must be said, for the conscience of the true scholar and the Christian teacher cannot be bound to human representations of truth, nor can the teacher so bind his students.

Liberty flourishes under neither totalitarianism nor anarchy, neither legalism nor license. It thrives under law, but is smothered in an atmosphere of fear and suspicion. Liberty is not uncommitted, but its commitment is to an ideal higher than current institutions or present laws. Academic freedom is valuable only when there is a prior commitment to the truth. And commitment to the truth is fully worthwhile only when that truth exists in One who transcends both the relativity of human perspectives and the fears of human concern.

Academic freedom may be defined, then, as freedom to explore the truth in a responsible fashion, to think, even to make mistakes and correct them; it is the freedom of the teacher to enlist students in the same quest, and to equip them carefully for its exacting demands; it is the freedom of the student to think for herself and to disagree on reasonable grounds with what her teachers say.

The qualifying words, "responsible" and "carefully," require emphasis, for it is here that educators are most often accused of failure. The qualification implies a responsible motive, neither selfish nor narrowly partisan, but first a love for the truth and then a concern for the common good of the community to which one belongs. It implies care about attitudes, lest one grow heady and opinionated and cease to bow in humility and awe. It implies working loyally within the framework of reference to which one stands committed, rather than acting like iconoclasts or teaching subversion. The teacher in the evangelical institution operates within the framework of belief confessed by his college. In this sense the academic community is always a community of the committed.

Academic freedom is a form of "liberty under law." Law gives order and direction to liberty, protecting it against abuses from right and from left, guiding and safeguarding its proper use. The Christian educator cannot forget that her responsibility is not only to society and the church, to her students and colleagues, but also and primarily to the truth. She is constantly impressed with the fact that the Scriptures aid rather than hinder the quest for truth: they open up new and exciting perspectives for the dedicated and vigorous mind to explore.

The apostle Paul spoke of Christian liberty in relation to the "weaker brother" (1 Cor. 8–9). To this weaker brother the Christian educator bears a dual responsibility. As an educator I must help him gain strength and maturity of faith and thought by offering fellowship and guidance in the exercise of liberty. Overprotection breeds weakness; repression breeds rebellion. As a Christian, however, I must not cause a weaker brother to stumble. I must not weaken him further, nor alienate him from the faith. In order to avoid becoming a stumbling-block I need to scrutinize my pedagogy, organize my curriculum, even restrict at times my own public utterances.

The customary distinction between academic and political freedom is important. What I say or do as a private citizen outside my own area of professional competence cannot be justified on the grounds of academic freedom. Nor does the American college desire the liberty intended by the German *Lehrfreiheit*, with its freedom to teach whatever I choose, whenever I choose, and however I choose. That may be proper in the German university but not with the structured curriculum and stated objectives of the American liberal arts college. Nor does academic freedom give the teacher the lectern to ride hobbies, to proselytize for peculiar viewpoints, or to engage in a knock-down drag-out fight with everyone who disagrees. On some matters I may wish to keep silent, to remain noncommital or to withhold judgment. In no case should I deliberately overstate my case or assert a degree of finality that the evidence does not justify. Responsibility and propriety require that freedom subserve the truth with complete honesty, and with loyalty to the goals of the institution a teacher serves.

There can be no skeletons in the closet, no significant alternatives ignored, no embarrassing questions barred. We need not restrict what can be taught; rather we should look at things in their historical and philosophical contexts and think in terms of worldviews and cultural outlooks. We must remember that Christianity touches learning not only at obvious points of theological contact, but in the interpretation of material. We need not excise dangerous things from the curriculum; rather we should build a curriculum and a methodology by means of which anything can be properly interpreted and profitably discussed, in which students progressively make truth and value judgments of their own. They will face it all after graduation anyway, perhaps earlier. It is a tragedy if in their bull sessions and campus publications students raise questions and air ideas with a frankness they do not experience in class, and if we encourage it in class it is inconsistent to restrict it outside. Improprieties may occur to embarrass us— but students are still immature late adolescents to whom propriety comes hard. Adolescents need frank discussion and patient guidance rather than restrictions whose unexplained or inconsistent inflexibility incites reactions and builds negative temperaments. To repress student freedom of thought and expression is like brainwashing; they should rather be inspired to channel their freedom into constructive Christian thought and action.

### PROBLEMS

Two kinds of criticism are leveled at the Christian college, one from the left and one from the right. From the left comes the charge that education from a religious perspective lacks objectivity and therefore respectability. But if intellectual objectivity is presuppositionless thinking or learning without guiding purposes, then it exists neither in the Christian college nor anywhere else. Neutrality on matters of belief and value is humanly impossible. Objectivity consists rather in acknowledging and scrutinizing one's point of view and testing presuppositions. It is more a matter of honesty than of neutrality. Every scholar has commitments. The Christian college is unique only because its faculty and administration have common commitments of a religious and moral sort, rather than the variegated commitments of a secular institution.

It is readily recognized in the literature on academic

freedom that responsibility to the truth, to scholarly integrity, and to one's students goes hand in hand with academic freedom. These are commitments made tacitly or explicitly by the university teacher, yet they are held to be quite consonant with freedom and objectivity. In the Christian college, additional theological commitments are often expected of the teacher, whether to an institutional or denominational statement of faith or in the form of his own credo, but these also are consonant with intellectual honesty and objectivity if the teacher is open about it and believes what he does thinkingly. Moreover, some such commitments are essential in defining the faith and making it a base from which to work at the integration of learning. The American Association of University Professors asks only that any such conditions of employment be clearly stated in writing at the time of appointment.[5]

Some church-related colleges establish no such conditions of employment, and look at them as negatively as political liberals looked at "loyalty oaths" in the McCarthy era. It is argued that, with the possible exception of its religion department, a Christian college should maintain the same religious pluralism as a public university. It would probably be wise not to have teachers openly antagonistic to the goals of the college, but otherwise even an atheist might hold a faculty position.

This viewpoint presupposes some other idea of a Christian college than that which I have been developing. It suggests including Christian beliefs and values into the curriculum as an addendum or perhaps a catalyst for Christian thought rather than as the motivational and informative center of an entire education. It does not envision bringing the creative contribution of Christian perspectives to bear in all disciplines and all campus activities. The elaboration of a coherent worldview and the development of college life as a Christian academic community would simply not be possible under such

5. See the American Association of University Professors' 1940 statement reprinted in *Academic Freedom and Tenure*, ed. Louis Joughin (University of Wisconsin Press, 1967), pp. 33-39.

an arrangement. This is not to say that it has no value at all, but rather that it comes in between the idea of an institute of Christian studies on a secular campus and an education expressive of the ultimate unity of truth in obedience to the creation mandate.

It is essential to recognize that a college is not a local church. The danger of subordinating education to indoctrination or moralizing or other activities finds an instructive parallel in the efforts of the 1960s to politicize the university. In that case the educational task was subordinated to political and social action as student groups attempted to force change. But to make the campus an arena for political action is as much a violation of the freedom to teach and to learn as it is to make the campus into an indoctrination center or even a missionary agency. Informed political and social concerns have their place in an educational institution, and Christian conviction and witness do for Christians in any setting, but a college is still a college and academic freedom protects its right to be primarily a place of learning.

This introduces the criticism from the right, that teachers and students use academic freedom as a license to compromise faith and morals, and that their freedom must therefore be either restricted or removed. Restrictions on freedom in general develop because our world as a whole, and the church in particular, is in trouble and life is not as free as it should be for any of us. In the attempt to conserve the accomplishments of the past, cherished social and religious institutions, and long-held particular viewpoints, or to enforce a viewpoint deemed essential for the present, there is a tendency to deny the freedom to improve on the past, to examine, to question, and to disagree.

This process is unfortunately aided by depreciating the academic task. Who has not encountered the hardheaded businessman who smiles indulgently at the educator's idealism? How many parents relish the fact that someone else is going to mold Junior's mind and help determine his destiny? How many parents fear that higher education will kill their son's faith? How many of us, set in our ways, like our unthinking passivity to be disturbed by some Socratic gadfly? Is it any wonder that some people try to swat the bugs that pester them?

Academic freedom would not create such criticism if we had ideal faculty, ideal students, ideal administrators, ideal trustees, and ideal constituencies. But this is not yet the best of all possible worlds. The truth can surely speak for itself to honest and mature and well-informed minds, but not all minds are equally honest and mature and well informed, and we are at best poor communicators.

Students are often raised on credulity, sometimes told it is dangerous to think and to question what they are taught. Their view of Christianity is oversimplified, their faith a response to the stimuli of parents and pastors; it is a sword they have yet to try and count on when they stand alone, embattled by new ideas and conflicting values. Is it any wonder that some falter, that others react against the naiveté or obscurantism they see or imagine in their backgrounds? Pedagogical care and curriculum revision alone cannot keep them from this, nor can restrictions on their freedom to read widely and to think for themselves, for now they are growing up and being invited to join the human race in their own right. Yet college is a place to think, to raise questions and doubts and discuss them openly, and the Christian college must encourage students to do so in dialog with more mature minds, and to confront the best information and arguments available.

Trustees may come from similar backgrounds, successful professionals and businessmen, properly respected for what they have accomplished in their own fields of endeavor. They may be well equipped to handle financial investments, well able to project institutional expansion, but in educational matters many of them remain novices. In some cases they earned no more than a baccalaureate degree; some less. Yet they are called upon to make strategic decisions affecting the educational work of the college. Their understanding of educational philosophy, the value they place on academic freedom, and their theological insight and balance are frequently impoverished. Unless a trustee chooses to withhold judgment, or takes the time and effort to think through educational philosophy and related issues, he will by default be prone to blunder, and not least in actions affecting academic freedom, its existence and its implementation. Public relations considerations sometimes conflict with educational considerations. An ill-informed decision is often worse than no decision at all.

This is a peculiar plight of the American college. German universities are state institutions, theoretically free from political domination, despite their spotty history. The British university is operated by the faculty themselves, who control every aspect of college life and work. Whether or not this is desirable, the facts of life for us are different, and these facts reinforce the sacred responsibility of all those concerned.

What can be done about it? It is time that evangelical educators took the initiative in educating the evangelical public as to the nature of Christian higher education and the role of academic freedom. A college is not a church. The educator's speeches and sermons and articles as well as the college's advertisements and catalogs and brochures could expound more eloquently than they do the idea of a Christian college and the responsible use to which it tries to put its freedom.

Administrators and trustees, moreover, must protect responsible freedom against attacks from right and left. They must stand by the professor under criticism and treat him with the highest personal and ethical consideration. They must ensure him at all times the respect and dignity that befits a man of integrity, a loyal citizen, a devout believer, a gentleman and a scholar. They must support the right of students to learn, to express their ideas, and to take reasoned exception to what they are told.

To this end it must be clearly recognized that intellectual gestation (to use Socrates's figure of midwifery), while unavoidably necessary and delightfully rewarding, can still be a dangerous and painful process. The incidence of miscarriages is to be reduced, not by further restriction on the attendant doctor, but by encouraging him to face facts honestly, to look into problems with the penetration of X-rays, to develop responsible techniques based on well-informed understanding and thoroughly critical research. Education, like having babies, is a calculated risk. Education is not like training: most children can be successfully trained, but not all babies are successfully delivered. Yet both education and having babies are part of the divine mandate to replenish and subdue the earth and have dominion in God's creation.

# 7 COLLEGE AS COMMUNITY

Traditionally, the American college operated *in loco parentis*, exercising authority over the personal lives as well as the academic pursuits of students in behalf of their parents. This concept became impracticable in the increasingly large universities of the mid-twentieth century, and increased emphasis on student rights along with precedent-setting court cases have brought it into question.

*In loco parentis* meant that American colleges accepted responsibility for all sides of student life. The Christian college has not abandoned that notion, but nowadays it is more often expressed in the idea of a college community. Involvement in the life of a community is a large part of what attracts students to small colleges, for faculty-student relations are often closer and opportunities for campus leadership, athletic participation, and such like are more readily available than in large universities. The Christian college, moreover, is largely a community of Christians whose intellectual and social and cultural life is influenced by Christian values, so that the learning situation is life as a whole approached from a Christian point of view. It is a situation calculated to teach young people to relate everything to their faith.

## THE IDEA OF COMMUNITY

A Christian community need not be an unrealistic environment, for as long as human beings, Christians included, are immature, fallible, and prone to sin, and as long as the college community maintains lively interaction with the non-Christian world, the campus remains far from any otherworldly utopia. To my mind, the main dangers facing a Christian college community are rather those confronting any community: excessive individualism and excessive administrative control.

Excessive individualists tend to behave like Robinson Crusoes, each on his own island trying to find himself by doing his own insular thing, as if it were possible for him in either life or thought to cut himself off from society. We are intrinsically social beings. The life of a hermit is less than human. Yet some tend to shun community by losing themselves in the anonymity of a large university, and some by noninvolvement in the religious, political, or social life of the campus. Some do so by closing their minds to other people's ideas. The person who treats the liberal arts as largely irrelevant chooses the life of an intellectual hermit. The person who regards the past as unrelated to his own life is a historical hermit, living in isolation from others. The person who values doing his own thing without regard for more universal and lasting values is an ethical hermit.

The opposite danger is that a college impose its ways on unwilling members, frustrating them as individuals and stunting their growth by forcing them into institutional patterns. Excessive controls occur in the political realm in totalitarian societies; they occur in the home in the case of unreasonably dictatorial parents who cannot let Johnny grow up and be himself; they would occur if a school prescribed dress codes, dormitory hours, and other behavioral standards in such a casuistical fashion as to leave no room for different life-styles or for individual choice. Both extremes exhibit a misunderstanding of the nature of human community and the social nature of individuals.

Seventeenth- and eighteenth-century philosophers sometimes talk as if a person is by nature an individualist who could lead a fully human life without social institutions, a Robinson Crusoe without intrinsic need for Friday or anyone else. The family and the state are not part of the created order, but rather a later product of individual self-interest accommodating itself to other people. On the other hand, Greek and Roman philosophers recognized that we are by nature social beings, and that this is inseparable from our rational nature. According to the Old Testament, God knew from the beginning that it was not good for us to be alone. Nobody can live with meaning entirely for herself. We are what we are and become what we become through the influence of parents, friends, schooling, church, and so on. Probably the peer group is the greatest single influence in shaping young people of high school and college age. But in any case we are social beings in our very nature, created to live in communion with God and community with other people.

A person develops intellectually in learning from others (and the dormitory "bull session" is often as important to her growth as the classroom). Her history is that of her society; her values are shaped by others and shape others in turn; she exercises her freedom with regard for the freedom of others. Because our rational and historical and valuational nature all require societal life, it follows that to develop those aspects of oneself a liberal education can best be conducted within a community.

Community arises from the social nature of those whose common stake in life and common values unite them in a common task. When a community organizes its life to preserve or enhance or transmit those values or to undertake its task more effectively, institutions arise. They are ordered communities with an outward structure of rules and procedures intended to implement an inner community of interest and purpose. We have institutions of various sorts: domestic, political, economic, and religious as well as educational. In any institution rules or laws are established to implement its goals while preserving the rights and furthering the interests of its members individually and collectively.

Individualism therefore becomes excessive when individuals without essential community of value and purpose fragment the life and frustrate the goals of an institution. Each must realize that we cannot achieve our ends in isolation from, or at cross-purposes with, the institutions of which we are part. Administrative controls become excessive when they no longer express any underlying community of interest and purpose nor allow for individual differences that are compatible with the common purpose.

## THE BASIS OF COMMUNITY

Campus talk often claims that love creates community, that unless people feel warmly toward each other all the time, there is no community. This is mistaken on two counts. First, it confuses love with feeling. Christian love is a moral virtue, not just, and sometimes not at all, a warm quality to one's feelings. It is the sort of moral concern for others' well-being that motivates hard and sacrificial work. What love does on the inward side of human relations, justice attempts on the outward side by securing people's rights and opportunities as equitably as possible. Love, then, is not community-feeling but an inner moral attitude and commitment.

Second, to say that love creates community, when "love" denotes liking and feeling, puts the cart before the horse. It is not feelings of love that create community, but community that creates feelings of love. Our likes and dislikes grow out of our experiences and for that reason feelings are fickle: they fluctuate up and down with health and digestion and climate and a myriad of other incidentals. But in working together at their marriage, a couple's feelings are nourished and grow; in working together in the life of a church, feelings of warmth and togetherness are enhanced; an athletic team will often talk of a feeling of oneness that grows out of shared experiences. And the feeling of community on campus is enriched when students, faculty, and administration are all heartily involved in their common educational task.

What does create a community if it is not common feeling? Community is created by values and purposes and a common task. Paul described the unity of the church with all its rich diversity of gifted individuals in terms of the faith and the mandate that gave the church reason to exist. What holds a marriage together are the values and goals a couple share, not primarily either their feelings or their marriage contract. The things that unite a nation are its common heritage and ideals. For we are reflective and valuing beings whose understanding and purposes guide the ways we participate with others.

The college is a community, an academic community. Its unifying task is education. How a student may feel about a teacher or administrator or about rules and requirements is secondary to his moral commitment to that task. I do not expect students to like everything about me or my courses or the college, but I do expect them to be committed to gaining an education. It is that which qualifies them as members of an academic community.

We do well to remind ourselves that as an academic community a Christian college is not a local church—although it is very appropriate that its students and teachers worship together. Nor is it an athletic or social club—although physical and social development have an important place. Nor is it a service agency—although people serve others in need both on and off campus. Nor is it a vocational training school—although liberal learning is excellent preparation for many a job and vocational preparation may well grow out of the liberal arts. The educational task is what creates the Christian college community; it, not chapel services or social service or athletics or dates or job training, is its overall purpose and reason for existence. The Christian college is of course a community of faith as well as learning, but the two are not disconnected; rather they are to be integrated so that faith gives direction and meaning to learning. The goal is still educational, and membership in a Christian college community presupposes commitment to that end.


## A CLIMATE OF FAITH AND LEARNING

When it comes to implementing this ideal, the college community must work at what Ordway Tead called a "*climate* of learning." In the Christian college this should be extended to a "climate of faith and learning." Centuries ago Plato inquired whether virtue can be taught, and decided that if virtue is a form of knowledge it can be taught like anything else. But a virtue is not just an idea; a positive Christian attitude toward liberal learning, while a virtue, is not a form of knowledge to be taught that simply. The instructional process cannot ensure it. Yet the climate of a community helps create attitudes and impart values. A community that reflects and speaks and prays about what it is trying to do, that structures its life accordingly and enjoys itself in the process, creates levels of expectation.

We need to ask how values are transmitted. Young people assimilate them more from example than precept, more from their peers than from their elders, and more by being involved than by being spectators. Values can be caught from the contagious example of a community at work, in this case a community of enthusiastic and well-equipped scholars who infect their students with a love for learning and involve them in disciplined work. As teachers inspire students and students infect other students, a climate of learning emerges.

The teacher is the key to a climate of learning. His teaching is his ministry. His enthusiasm about ideas, his scholarship, and the importance he places on teaching provide a model. The Christian college has escaped the "publish or perish" syndrome, but this never justifies the opposite extreme of abandoning creative intellectual work. The teacher must keep up in his field and be involved in professional organizations; to grow he needs to expand his knowledge by research. Given the ability, the Christian professor has the same moral responsibility as other scholars to publish in his field, along with the added responsibility of developing Christian perspectives when they are pertinent to what he writes. His example helps create a climate of faith and learning in the college community.

Teaching is an exacting art that requires physical health, emotional balance, and mental acumen. The teacher of all people must therefore steward his personal resources for the job. His most disagreeable task—grading papers—is often one of the most important things he does. Grading has two purposes, evaluation and criticism. Evaluation is for the record that graduate schools and employers examine. Criticism is for the student's education. A paper that takes a student's time and best abilities deserves careful analysis. Detailed annotations and constructive suggestions will push him further than he previously thought possible and can sometimes teach him more than he learned from writing the paper in the first place.

It is important that the teacher be transparently Christian as well as an enthusiastic and careful scholar, and that he not compartmentalize the two but think integrationally himself. How he contributes to the campus climate may vary, for pedagogy is in large measure relative to personality, and lecturing can excite and involve the student as effectively as discussions and coffee hours, as long as it is not a substitute for careful student interaction with source materials. It is the person of the teacher rather than a particular gimmick or method that counts. As in Philips Brooks's classic definition of preaching, so too teaching conveys "truth through personality."

A community that argues ideas only in the classroom, a teacher whose work seems a chore, a student who never reads a thing beyond what is assigned, a campus that empties itself of life and thought all weekend, an attitude that devaluates disciplined study in comparison with rival claimants on time and energy, a dominant concern for job-preparation— these can never produce a climate of learning.

In his *Republic*, Plato urges selectivity in the use of literature and the arts because they too transmit values. We need not agree with Plato's censorship to realize that when a good writer involves her readers or a good artist captures her audiences she makes them feel as well as know the values she expresses. Exciting art and literature are like a captivating teacher in the effect they have on students; they too can generate a love of learning.

So can the college chapel service that is a regular part of community life in the Christian college. It should not be peripheral to the educational task but should constantly renew the vision of a Christian mind. When the well-intentioned speaker discourages intellectual pursuits or cultural involvements or political action, he turns off many students. Chapel speakers should realize that a Christian college exists to cultivate the intellect and involve people in their culture, and that it is therefore more than a conserving influence in the world. A college is Christian in that it does its work in a Christian way, not by encouraging an unthinking faith to counterbalance faithless thought. If education is God's present calling to students, then no question arises about whether God or studies come first, for God is to be honored in and through studies. Compartmentalization has no place on the Christian campus.

A college chapel service that renews this vision and keeps things in focus is essential in cultivating a climate of faith and learning. It is the college community at worship, cultivating Christian devotion, dedicating all its activities to the glory of God, seeking biblical instruction that will guide its life and thought, and reflecting on its God-given calling.

Values are also assimilated and lessons learned in extracurricular activities, whether journalistic, athletic, political, or religious. Each can make its own contribution and afford opportunities for growth. Unfortunately, they can also be educationally counterproductive if they are conducted in unthinking and irresponsible ways. They can turn their backs on the critical scrutiny that prevails in the classroom, as if it were irrelevant in "real life." Political groups can campaign in "single-issue" manner, dogmatizing rhetorically without really examining the positions they endorse or condemn; the campus newspaper, by ignoring political or artistic interests, makes negative judgments about their importance. Christian service activities often reinforce sixth-grade theological half-concepts and bad high school habits of speech. A Christian liberal arts education cannot be impounded in classrooms and libraries, but must extend itself into the extracurricular. Reflection on goals and methods, ideas and language are needed there too, along with careful value judgments. If students are to mature as responsible agents in all areas of life, linkages must be forged to make the extracurricular educational too.

The climate of faith and learning is also affected by college rules. Every institution has them, and necessarily so for its orderly and effective operation, and for the safeguarding of individual interests. But they need to be formulated and frequently reexamined with reference to overall educational goals. The primary purpose of a Christian college is not to insulate and protect students, but to educate them as responsible Christians. On the one hand, protection from bad influences is an unrealistic goal in a society where alcohol and drug abuse are widespread and sexual license is rampant. Most of our new students have already had to face all that far more directly than they will on Christian college campuses. On the other hand paternalistic protection is not really desirable with young adults about to launch out on their own. They must learn to use their freedom responsibly. The question about college regulations and their applications is, How do they contribute to this? Do they contribute to a climate of faith and learning that supports careful reflection, reinforces appropriate values, and encourages responsible action, and do they do so in a manner appropriate to the age and experience of our students?

A community, be it family or church or college, is perhaps the single most powerful influence in shaping a person's values. It is therefore of major importance that we shape that community well.

# 8 EXPERIENCE IS NOT ENOUGH

The young adult who graduates from a liberal arts college is a different person from the awkward high schooler who entered four years before. College can provide a wealth of experiences, and these are a catalyst for growth.

Living in a residence hall with scores of other young people makes demands on sociability, self-discipline, and concentration. Adjusting to a roommate whose different habits grate and annoy can so tax patience as to uncover flaws in one's own character. The relative independence of college learning and the pressure of deadlines call for habits of time management that do not yet exist. Participation in athletics will stretch energies and hone physical skills to a degree the player had never thought possible.

College is a time of growth, of self-discovery, of learning by trial and error, of finding out the hard way how to get along with other people and how to handle responsibility. Experience can be a great teacher.

Experiential education has expanded in recent years. Field trips and labs we have had for a long time, providing personal observation and hands-on experience of what otherwise would remain remote and just theoretical. Internships for psychology, pre-law, and many other students are now commonplace. Stress programs are encouraged that require both teamwork and solitary self-reliance in some remote wilderness. And foreign study–travel can be enjoyed for academic credit. What is really the educational worth of all this?

Education is made for people, not people for education. Because a person is more than a worker, a wage earner, we insist that vocational training is not enough. Similarly a person is not just an intellect, assimilating knowledge and gaining cognitive skills. We are also affective and social beings, and these dimensions of personality have to grow too if one is to become an effective and responsible person. Consider the provincialisms that have to be overcome, even chauvinism and bigotry. Seeing how other people live, realizing that the American way of life and American-style politics are not the only viable ones, identifying for a while with ghetto dwellers, working as a male nursing assistant in a hospital—all of this can make a very worthwhile contribution.

Consider also that moral development is not a purely cognitive affair but is affective as well. I have to interiorize the love I should give. I have to hunger and thirst for social justice. Coming face to face with human need and feeling the frustration of victims of injustice can help. And wrestling with some of the moral dilemmas created by the complexities of modern society can help us live with ambiguity, as often an adult must. Experience contributes an affective dimension to learning.

But is that enough? I think not.

## PRAGMATISM IN EXPERIENTIAL EDUCATION

In the first place, the development of experience-oriented education has been deeply influenced by an instrumentalist philosophy of education in the tradition of John Dewey. The term "experience," for Dewey, denotes the total reality of life, the basic nature of human existence. Experience is an immersion in natural processes, our sense of security challenged by unforeseen problems which demand solution. Learning therefore is elicited by problem situations. The ideas we come up with are simply hypotheses for solving them. The things we value are temporary: we value them because they are threatened, and so we try to think of ways to preserve them. All learning is therefore situational. We build up a fund of experience on which to draw, but there are no universal values, no fixed truths, no absolutes. Learning is learning to adjust. Even the classroom simulates life experiences, rather than exploring a heritage of truth and values.

This philosophy was, in Dewey's thinking, simply an application of the theory of natural selection. While that foundation may not be in mind in all experience-oriented learning, it nonetheless reminds us to scrutinize our own presuppositions. If there are fixed truths and eternal values, if there is an objective order to the creation, and if God's purposes for us are significant, then a purely situational approach to learning breaks down. Experience is not enough.

In effect, this brings us back to the educational model with which we began in Chapter 3. We are educating responsible agents. Prerequisite to responsible action are reflection and valuing. This means bringing the resources of the disciplines to experience, encouraging internships *after* being introduced to related disciplines, internships *followed by* careful consideration of theoretical and ethical assumptions and their consequences, internships that *lead to* an agenda for more thorough study. Experience, to be fully educational, needs historical, theoretical, scientific, and ethical input and scrutiny.

## THE LIMITATIONS OF EXPERIENCE

In the second place, to suppose unanalyzed experience itself is an omnicompetent teacher presupposes an empiricist theory of knowledge that is nowadays highly suspect. The eighteenth century view that we can gather piecemeal data and come up with generalizations and causal explanations simply has not stood up under scrutiny. Empirical observation is not entirely objective but selective, guided by theoretical assumptions and personal interests. This has become evident in recent work on the history of science: and if experience is not enough for science, how can it be enough for education?

To make the case as obvious as possible, I offer a simple syllogism:

> Experience alone is not understanding.
> Education requires understanding.
> Therefore experience alone is not education.

The *first premise*, "experience alone is not understanding," has a familiar ring to anyone acquainted with the history of philosophy, for Plato went into great detail in his *Theaetetus* to show that this is so. Perception is not knowledge, he argued, for perceptual experience varies with the observer's physical and psychological condition. It makes a difference whether we are tired or fresh, attentive or confused, close to or distant from an object, in front of it or beside it. A coin, for instance, is seen as circular, elliptical, or a straight line, depending on the vantage point of the observer. A dog hears a whistle pitched too high for the human ear. It also makes a difference when objects of experience change and, as Plato pointed out, all physical things change in some way. The tree outside my window looks different in October than in December and again in April or May. People change, and so do political structures and social mores. We cannot base unchanging knowledge on changing experience of changing things. Experience yields none of the lasting truth that understanding seeks.

Such is Plato's argument. As a rationalist he may have underestimated the contribution of experience to understanding, but he is nonetheless correct about the changeableness and relativity of human experience. I therefore moderate his conclusion by adding the word "alone," and affirm that experience *alone* is not enough.

Another classic problem was exhibited by David Hume. Experience is always limited in scope: we have our present experience, but we do not now experience the past in the same way we did, nor do we yet experience the future. How can we know what lies beyond our present experience? Yet we need to if we are to learn from the past and plan for the future. And we claim to know more than our present experience every time we generalize. Some scientific theories are of this sort, generalizations based on present and past experience and applicable to future experience. In fact the predictive power of a scientific theory is one of its principal virtues. Yet Hume pointed out that generalizations can be drawn from present experience only by assuming the uniformity of nature. But that is the very point at stake, namely that the future is like the present and the past. It seems, then, that empirical generalizations are without logical grounds: they rest on generalizations about uniformity that experience itself can never finally establish. However we broaden our observations and enrich our sensitivities, the same problem persists. Experience alone is not enough to support the generalized understanding that education seeks.

A third problem, posed by Immanuel Kant, is of particular interest to Christians. Experience is not self-interpreting. The word "interpretation" is another can of worms: it can mean (a) the discovery of causes and consequences, (b) exploring conceptual relations, or (c) making value judgments. But whichever way we take it, we have to introduce assumptions that experience alone cannot establish. In the case of (a) we introduce the idea of cause and effect; in regard to (b) we employ various kinds of logical relationship; in (c) we need some idea of right and wrong or good and bad. None of these assumptions, Kant argued, is derived from experience: they are rather the presuppositions of intelligible experience. Kant regarded them as universal and necessary. I am inclined to regard many of them more as part of an underlying worldview that we bring to experience. Even then interpretation depends on presuppositions, and if they vary from one worldview to another, our interpretations will too.

The Christian educator should realize that the presuppositions one brings to experience, be they Christian or non-Christian, shape the understanding. Experience is not self-interpreting. For example, the French Catholic existentialist Gabriel Marcel and the French atheistic existentialist Jean-Paul Sartre interpret interpersonal relationships very differently. In his play *A Man of God*, Marcel finds a glimmer of faith and love and hope where Sartre in *No Exit* finds only negation and absurdity. Again, the 1960s student radical who followed Herbert Marcuse in tracing his unhappy experience to modern economic structures adopted Marcuse's neo-Marxist presuppositions about economic causation in history.

My point is that if understanding seeks unchanging truth that covers a variety of changing moods and experiences

(Plato's problem), if understanding requires generalization beyond our present experience (Hume's problem), if understanding involves interpretation and evaluation (Kant's problem), then experience alone is not the same as understanding and our first premise is established.

The *second premise* is that education requires understanding or, to be more precise, the goals of liberal education do. Here again we must distinguish liberal education from its neighbors. It is not synonymous with training, which develops skills; nor is it the same as indoctrination, which imposes information with a view to unquestioning assent. Training and indoctrination seek to determine student behavior, but liberal education prepares for the wise exercise of freedom through the develoment of understanding. Nor is liberal education to be equated with a general education that ensures breadth. General education tries to overcome the limited scope of ordinary experience and knowledge, but liberal education is concerned not only with broad scope but also with seeing things as an interrelated whole, therefore with understanding truth and value, with presuppositions that help us interpret experience and make reasonable value judgments. My point is that by definition if we are engaged in liberal education we have to develop the understanding, and our second premise is established.

The *conclusion* follows: if experience alone is not understanding and if education requires understanding, then experience alone is not enough for education.

### EXPERIENCE AS EDUCATIONAL

In God's world, the Christian should obviously value experience and feeling and emotion as well as understanding. Learning should touch the real issues we experience rather than detach itself like a remote game of chess. My proposal is simply that experience can be educati*onal* even if by itself it is not education. Experience and education are still related: even though experience sometimes plays the chauvinist husband and tries to run Frau Education, it is in reality more like the proverbial mother-in-law. That is, she constantly intrudes on education's life; sometimes she tries to dominate, sometimes she provokes and irritates, but always she offers valuable material for thought and she remains much loved. Education can never push experience wholly out of her life; nor should she, for they are members of the same family.

The relationship is of course based on the fact that both can contribute to persons. In relation to education, experience contributes vastly: it motivates by capturing interest and attention, it illuminates by providing points of reference in the lived-world, it provides raw material for the processes of interpretation, it breaks down prejudices, it stimulates the imagination. The experience of living in the ghetto illustrates this: it can be fascinating enough to interest the student in a serious study of urban problems; the firsthand encounter will make generalized and theoretical material seem concrete and realistic; for a long time thereafter the perplexities and ambiguities of the situation will cry out for explanation and resolution; and it will stimulate all sorts of ideas as to what can be done to change the situation.

During the latter part of the Vietnam conflict, I offered a course called "The Morality of War." Student feelings ran high and provided motivation; current events and the experience of frustration and ambiguity illuminated the historical and philosophical materials under study. More important, a careful examination of the historical development of pacifism and the just war theory and a discussion of ethical, political, and legal philosophy provided a sense of history and a theoretical basis for interpreting and evaluating current events reasonably rather than just "sounding off" about them. In that context, experience was educational.

But unexamined experience—what we have variously called "experience alone" and "raw experience"—is not enough, for it is not fully enough human. It must be humanized if it is to be educational, so what has been said about the nature of persons will again help us.

A person is a reflective being, a valuing being, and a responsible agent. In the first place, then, the *experience of rational activity* can be educational. As a philosophy teacher I have to ask what experiences could contribute significantly to philosophical education. Careful consideration of the moral questions posed by war could well do so, but not just the physical and emotional stress of going to war or of resisting it unanalytically and without theoretical basis. I do not think that a student's untutored reflections on his experience in physical stress programs merit either philosophy or psychology credit: philosophy and psychology should be far more scientific than that. A European travel program would be enriching in many ways, but seeing the carved figure of St. Anselm outside Canterbury Cathedral contributes little to my understanding or appreciation of his ontological argument, and visiting the Sorbonne does not itself enable me to wrestle more effectively with Bergson or Sartre. Of course it would add local color and help to discuss their thinking with them at length but then, granted the possibility of resuscitation, it would be a lot easier and cheaper to fly them over here than for a crowd of us to go over there. Plainly, the experience of philosophical reasoning that contributes to philosophical education can be secured as effectively on campus as off. The educational value of European travel programs is more in fields like history and art than in philosophy.

Old ways of teaching did not always work. To lecture and examine over three or four classical positions on each of eight or nine classical problems, along with two or three classical arguments for each of the three or four classical positions about eight or nine classical problems may produce only a boring recital of annotated grocery lists. Essential to philosophical education is the experience of wrestling for oneself with problems and arguments and positions. Papers and discussions accordingly serve in philosophy as a ghetto experience might in sociology or a laboratory experience in the teaching of science; and this says something about the maximum size of philosophy classes. But papers and discussions without sufficient historical and theoretical and logical input and without painstaking criticism, while quite an experience, easily deteriorate into a trivial parading of ignorance. Experience alone is not education; to be educational it must involve informed and self-critical rational activity. As Kant reminded us, understanding requires both empirical and rational input.

In the second place, the *experience of making reasonable value judgments* can be educational, for it contributes to the development of a valuing being. Here again we must remember that values are not just feelings. A value judgment is the application to an individual case of aesthetic or moral or political or religious principles. The experience must therefore involve the formulation as well as the application of such principles, not in an emotionless fashion, but with sufficient detachment to be able to appraise the way we feel as well as to appraise the principles and cases in question. Sometimes our feelings will have to be brought into line with our value judgments, for feeling must ultimately conform to the truth rather than the truth conforming to however we may feel.

One art teacher I know complains that his students cannot verbalize why they feel as they do about art works, let alone formulate principles of aesthetic judgment on which to base their art criticism. To the extent that a student cannot think his way into such matters (not necessarily "through" them), he is not educated in art, but only trained. His experience is not educational unless he learns how to make defensible value judgments in his field of endeavor.

This suggests that the educational value of living in the ghetto lies not just in getting the "feel" of urban and minority problems, but rather in the experience of making well-informed and reasoned value judgments. It is not enough that the student says what she personally thinks and feels about school busing, an assignment that can engender triviality and relativism, but that she explores the viability of alternative evaluations in relation not only to the observable facts but also to the assumptions various social scientists and ethicists and theologians make about human nature and behavior. The positivist social scientist will not like this, but the Christian should by now have paid parting compliments to positivism and come to see the impact of theological and ethical and methodological assumptions on both thought and behavior. Christian education requires that the student gain experience in detecting assumptions, in clarifying presuppositions, and in making value judgments accordingly. Too easily "field experience" can forget what should have been done in "theoretical" courses, and become entirely pragmatic.

In the third place, we are responsible agents, and *educational experience may profitably involve significant activities* of our own and other people. This includes the historical, not cramming endless facts about the past but rather reliving it empathetically so as to understand the present and participate in shaping hypothetical directions for the future.

Travel experience does not automatically guarantee this sense of history and of cultural and social involvement. The ex-G.I. who refers to ancient ruins in Italy as old rocks about which he could not care less, had travel experience but no historical experience. He gave no evidence of the educated person's understanding and appreciation of the Roman heritage in law and politics and art symbolized by "old rocks," a heritage that has shaped our present and influenced the contours of a future to which we now have the responsibility of giving specific shape. Travel experience needs input concerning political and economic and artistic and religious concepts and values if it is to be of educational worth. Experience alone is not enough.

Similar observations might be made about internships and extracurricular activities. To be educational they must be conducted under the scrutiny of appropriate disciplines and with the input of theoretical and valuational and historical considerations. It is counterproductive educationally to sponsor activities, even Christian service activities, in which the student relapses into unreflective ways, or reflects without the scrutiny of a properly equipped mentor. What science teacher would dream, except in his wildest nightmares, of turning students loose in the laboratory without adequate preparation and without the collateral benefits of more theoretical and perhaps historical approaches to phenomena?

Liberal education develops the person. It is an open invitation to join the human race. Christian liberal arts education is an invitation to become increasingly a Christian person. But neither the excitement of traveling in Europe, nor the trauma of living in a ghetto, nor simply looking at paintings or making them, nor unexamined religious experience and service activities can develop an educated person. Experience must be humanized if it is to be educational; to be humanized it must be educated. In the final analysis that is why raw experience is not enough; uneducated experience cannot educate. Experience alone is not education.

# 9 THE MARKS OF AN EDUCATED PERSON

It was years ago now, when I had more idealism but less experience. An outside evaluation team had been assessing our department, and its senior member sat in my office to report what he thought about us. He had taught in major universities as well as a first-rate Christian college, earning a superb reputation as a scholar, a teacher, and an educational statesman. I was listening, perhaps more eager for plaudits than for complaints. "What kind of student do you want to come out of here?" he asked.

For all our stated objectives, I frankly thought more about the kind of student I wanted to come *into* my classes than qualities I wanted in those who went *out*. I suppose it seemed like a given that if they came to me with the right stuff they would automatically turn out just fine. But for the first time now I was forced to consider seriously what kind of person I hoped to see graduate, and to start from there in considering courses and pedagogy. What are the marks of an educated person?

Picture with me three individuals: Mary, Tom, and Pat.

Mary steps right out of college into exactly the job she has prayed without ceasing for through the past four years. She has given it all her energies—her major, her electives, her extracurricular activities, her work experience—all these she has concentrated singlemindedly to develop the skills she now will use. Nothing else really interests her and, besides, she's not really equipped for anything else. Is Mary an educated person? Is she not rather *trained* than educated? And in a rapidly changing economy, how long will it be before her job skills are outmoded?

Tom is popular, socially successful. He seems to get along well with everyone. He's handsome, gracious, polite, suave, well adjusted, well accepted—even though some people feel he subtly manipulates them. Every inch a WASP, he meets every social expectation, and of course he has personal ambition. He is active with the Young Republicans, and wants to run for office when he gets enough of a following. He even goes to church with some regularity. Is Tom an educated person? Is he not rather a socal *conformist,* a climber, than an educated man?

Pat has discovered things in college she never dreamed of before. It has opened her eyes to windows in every direction. It has sharpened her mind, heightened her imagination, deepened her understanding, broadened her sympathies, kindled new interests. A whole range of her capacities have been developed—aesthetic, intellectual, spiritual, social—that make her feel part of the whole human race. She is eager to shoulder her share of the load of human responsibility, and is ready to keep on learning to that end. Is Pat an educated person? Not Mary, not Tom, but Pat?

### THE PURPOSE OF EDUCATION

Why do we choose Pat? To answer that question, let me introduce another friend of mine, a Greek, an ancient, a philosopher. Aristotle claimed that education should prepare a person for an active life marked by excellence. Translators usually render his conception of the good life as "fulfillment" or "self-actualization," but taken by themselves these terms are terribly misleading. In contemporary idiom, "fulfilment" is a feeling of satisfaction; for Aristotle it was an achievement, a fact. Nowadays, "self-actualization" sounds individualistic, even self-centered, concerned about my own ideosyncratic possibilities; for Aristotle it represents the full actualization of my generically human capacities in the activities of this life.

Excellence, then, applies not to how we feel about ourselves, nor to how individualistic we become, but to the *quality* of my life, to its virtues. Intense pleasure may be the excellence appropriate to lower animals. But in humans excellence is found by a moral and intellectual development that guides my decisions and actions.

Develop yourself, he says, not just as a farmer or a physician or a businessman, but as a human being. Be reflective and be moral in everything you do. Become a thoroughly responsible agent. That is the mark of an educated person.

John Gardner points out that excellence shows itself in many ways.[1]

> Confucius teaches the feudal lords to govern wisely.
> Lincoln writes his second inaugural, "with malice toward none."
> Mozart composes his first oratorio at the age of eleven.
> Galileo drops weights from the Tower of Pisa.
> Emily Dickinson jots her "letters to the world" on odd scraps of paper.
> Florence Nightingale nurses the wounded in the Crimea.
> Eli Whitney pioneers the manufacture of interchangeable parts.
> Ruth says to Naomi, "Thy people shall be my people."

What do all these people have in common? They are human beings using their God-given gifts well. And excellence for Aristotle is that kind of quality in every area of one's life.

Let us pause at this juncture to get our theological bearings. The Christian, I suggest, makes three claims about this kind of ideal.

(1) Because we are creatures of God, made in his image, our highest end is to glorify God, and this includes the responsible stewardship of our entire lives. God's goal for us in education is thereby akin to Aristotle's active life marked by excellence.

(2) Because of God's grace, common grace restraining evil and saving grace that frees us from the bondage of sin, we approach this calling with realistic hopes. When Francis

---

1. John W. Gardner, *Excellence* (Harper Colophon Books, 1961), p. 130.

Bacon asserted that "knowledge is power," he explained that it can give us the ability to overcome some ill-effects of the fall. Said John Milton, "the end of learning is to repair the ruins of our first parents, by regaining to know God aright,"[2] and "I call a complete and generous education that which fits a man to perform justly, skilfully and magnanimously all the offices, both private and public, of peace and war."[3]

(3) Because God's kingdom of Shalom is already among us and yet to come in its fulness, education will concern itself with matters of justice, peace and love in this world, so as to help produce responsible agents rather than mere spectators on the events and social evils of our times.

These observations point us beyond Aristotle. What qualities should we then expect and work for in education?

## THE MARKS OF AN EDUCATED CHRISTIAN

From a Christian standpoint, motivating and giving direction to all else are what we shall call "spiritual virtues": an unreserved commitment to God and his purposes for us in this world, a confidence in the gospel, and a self-giving devotion—these which the apostle calls faith, hope, and love. They bring to the life of the mind purposefulness, expectation, humility.

Second are moral virtues, qualities of character like love and fairness, the courage of one's convictions, a thoroughgoing integrity, and a commitment to justice and love in every area of life.

These first two marks are expected of Christians in any context, but they are nonetheless concerns of the Christian college. It is with a third kind, however, that we reach a distinctive of education, qualities of mind that Aristotle would have included among his intellectual virtues: breadth of understanding, openness to new ideas, intellectual honesty about other views and about the problems in one's own, analytic and

---

2. "Of Education," *Complete Poetry and Selected Prose of John Milton* (Modern Library, 1942), p. 664.
3. "Of Education," p. 667.

critical skills, not just verbal skills and powers of communication but grace and eloquence therein as well, the ability to say the right thing in the right way at the right time—not only in business reports, sermons, and obituaries, but also in family life, in constructive conversation, in meeting strangers. Qualities of mind should include a sense of history, an imagination that frees us to work at both old and new problems in fresh ways, and to ask fresh questions; and a wisdom that gets down to basic principles, spotting assumptions and seeing what they entail, seeing what is right and good and true, and making sound decisions accordingly.

Said John Henry Newman:

> To open the mind, to correct it, to refine it, to enable it to know and to digest, master, and use its knowledge, to give it power over its own faculties, application, flexibility, method, critical exactness, sagacity, resource, address, eloquent expression, is an object . . . as intelligible as the cultivation of moral virtue. . . .[4]

But moral and intellectual virtues are not enough, for valuing and reflective beings are also responsible agents. We must add then a fourth set of qualities, those of responsible action in all areas of life: conscientiousness, helpfulness, a servantly but not servile manner, decisiveness, self-discipline, persistence, the ability to correct one's course and start afresh, to maintain good family relations, active involvement in church and community, to be an effective agent of needful and helpful change.

Finally, the qualities of self-knowledge: an honest appraisal of our own strengths and weaknesses, no false modesty and no overconfidence, a willingness to address those weaknesses and do something about them, and an equal willingness to invest one's strengths. Knowing oneself means knowing what has to be learned, knowing how I can go at learning it, and the ability to learn from others.

We begin to see now why we tend to choose Pat as an educated person. Let me say a little more about her.

---

4. J. H. Newman, *The Idea of a University* (Holt, Rinehart and Winston, 1960), pp. 92-93.

Pat is widely read. She has read Plato and Augustine, Shakespeare and William Faulkner. She's acquainted with both Bach and Bartók, and enjoys Monet and Picasso. She thinks of them all as her friends. But she does not brag: she wears these friendships lightly.

Pat is alert to the issues of the day: she feels the injustices of apartheid and admits there are ambiguities in Nicaragua. She listens to the other side, rather than reacting with an outburst of ridicule or anger. She measures her judgments before she acts, and before she votes. Her vote, in the end, is the kind of vote a democracy needs—informed, principled, and caring—not just blindly partisan. Her friends tell me she always gets to the heart of an issue.

Pat is aware of some new developments in science and technology, biology in particular, and the moral dimensions of genetic research both intrigue and concern her greatly—even though her major was literature. She continues to read, to learn, to grow, for she realizes that however large the circumference of her knowledge, just as large are the borders of her ignorance. Yet she doesn't worship either knowledge, or art, or influence, or even her relationships with her friends. She worships the One from whom all blessings flow, the One who gives but also takes away. Whatever her abilities, whatever her development, whatever her accomplishments, she blesses the name of the Lord.

Pat, I say, is an educated person.